DR BOB WOODW[illegible] Gloucester, United [illegible] ied at state and Stei[illegible] co-worker at the Sh[illegible] bury, a centre of the [illegible] Community, based on the teachings of Rudolf Steiner (1861-1925). He remained within the Camphill Movement, living with and teaching children with special educational needs, for some forty years, retiring in 2012. He took a special interest in understanding autism in children and young people.

At the age of 46, Bob received a M.Ed. degree from Bristol University, followed by a M.Phil. at the age of 50 and a Ph.D. from the University of the West of England at the age of 64. As well as being a qualified educator, he is a spiritual healer and the author of several books. He is married with five grown-up children and many grandchildren.

By the same author:

Spirit Healing (2004)
Spirit Communications (2007)
Spiritual Healing with Children with Special Needs (2007)
Trusting in Spirit – The Challenge (2018)
Knowledge of Spirit Worlds and Life After Death (2020)
Journeying Into Spirit Worlds (2022)

Autism – A Holistic Approach
(with Dr Marga Hogenboom) (3rd edition 2013)

KARMA
IN HUMAN LIFE

As received through spirit guides

Dr Bob Woodward

CLAIRVIEW

Clairview Books Ltd.,
Russet, Sandy Lane,
West Hoathly,
W. Sussex RH19 4QQ

www.clairviewbooks.com

Published by Clairview Books 2022

A CIP catalogue record for this book is available from the British Library

ISBN 978 1 912992 40 9

Cover by Morgan Creative
Typeset by Symbiosys Technologies, Visakhapatnam, India
Printed and bound by 4Edge Ltd, Essex

CONTENTS

ACKNOWLEDGEMENTS

Many thanks to my friend Michael Allen, who offered to take my handwritten manuscript and transcribe it into clear print. He did this task for me in record time!

Thanks also to Sevak Gulbekian, Editor-in-Chief, and the team at Clairview for being so willing to consider my new text for publication.

Thank you to both Viktoria and Pete for reading the manuscript and giving me such positive, independent feedback. Pete then very kindly wrote the Foreword.

Lastly, my gratitude to the nine guides who stepped forward to give the teachings and then also to respond to my questions on the various chapter themes. Clearly, it is only possible to do this form of spiritual research work when those who live on the 'other side' of life agree to cooperate with those of us who are still incarnated on the earth.

So, once again, my heartfelt thanks to all my spirit guides.

FOREWORD

Karma for most of us is best understood as 'cause and effect', relating to our daily interactions with others. Bob's book seeks to show that karma is not so easily explained, or to be seen in such black-and-white terms. It is much more complex and interwoven with past-life situations that play a part in our current earthly lives. It also relates to some of the great puzzles of our time, such as the causes of pandemics and illnesses, wars and climate change.

Bob, rightly, trusts his wonderful spirit guides and lets them have pride of place. There are many books on this subject that may well be more detailed. But Bob's book gives us new insight into this complex subject, and leaves the door open for his formidable guides to provide yet more depth of understanding in future books. I, for one, look forward to these!

Peter John
Psychic Artist

1.
INTRODUCTION

I put the following question to Joshua Isaiah, my main spirit guide, in October 2019:

Bob: Joshua, I am wondering about the possibility of working with the guides (see Appendix) on a book which addresses questions within the theme of 'karma', and how this plays out in human life. How the so-called 'law of karma' or, perhaps, 'karmic laws', work within the relationships and connections that we make in living out our lives on earth. Would such a project be something that you and the other guides would be willing to work with me on? What do you think, Joshua?

I received the following answer:

Joshua: Bob, my friend, we would be very happy to undertake such a task with you, because we realize that, through this theme of karma, many important questions would be raised, and that light can start to be thrown upon many puzzles and enigmas of life on earth. So, yes, my friend, we can work with you on this project if this is what you decide to do. The choice is yours, but as such, we are more than willing to work with you on this important theme. All blessings, Joshua.

Bob: Right, Joshua, thank you. But do all the guides that I know so far wish to contribute to this, or only some of them? Or, would perhaps new guides emerge to step forward and contribute?

Joshua: My friend, let us see how this work develops. Simply be open to see who wishes to step forward and make a contribution. Be open, shall we say, to the guides who are there to help with this theme and project.

Bob: Right, Joshua, so in a way this will be another test of my trust in working with the guides, right?

Joshua: My friend, you can certainly look at it like that, but in reality we do not have any doubts that you are prepared to put your trust in us. You have already proved this by all our previous work. However, let's see how things develop if you decide to undertake this task, and see then how it evolves. A work in progress, so to speak.

Bob: Yes, Joshua, I will be very interested to see how it evolves, as you say, once we actually get going with it. Many thanks. Actually, Joshua, I have just listed the themes for each chapter. What do you think of these?

Joshua: Yes, my friend, this is something we can work with. As I said before, be open to see how things develop when we work together. All blessings, Joshua.

Bob: Joshua, just one further question about the format. Would it be good if one or another guide first stepped forward to give a teaching for each chapter, then followed by a Q and A session? Would this be a good format, or alternatively, should we just do each chapter on a Q and A basis, with me being open to whoever wants to contribute? What do you feel is best?

Joshua: Shalom, my friend. We think it is best to give a teaching first, then followed up by your questions, where whoever wishes to step forward to give an answer would do so. This is our suggestion as to how best to proceed.

Bob: Right, Joshua, I can go along with that. Thank you.

*

Thereafter, I began work on this new research project with the guides, and completed four chapters by November of that year. However, there I stopped, though I cannot now recall the reason for this. It may well have been due to some outer life circumstances.

Now, two years later, in November 2021, I am ready to resume this task, and to see what knowledge the guides can give us on this theme. If, as I understand from my studies of Rudolf Steiner's anthroposophy, the laws of karma affect and encompass all areas of our human lives, then understanding how they work is really important. Through such understanding, we may be better equipped to make sense of the various enigmas, issues and challenges which we all experience.

While the basic idea of 'karma' is not new – having long been a central feature of Eastern spirituality and religious traditions – the details of how it works encompass differing concepts. Can the guides give us a true knowledge of it, maybe separating out the wheat from the chaff? If so, can we apply this practically and helpfully to the challenges of our everyday lives? Let us hope so!

Given all that has dramatically taken place in the world since I first started this project, the whole subject seems to me even more relevant now. Can it, for example, throw light on the global coronavirus pandemic, maybe its causes and significance in the twenty-first century? Also, light on the even bigger challenge of global warming and climate change, which are being discussed at the COP26* conference

---

*On a yearly basis, the United Nations has been holding a global climate change conference known as a COP, which stands for 'Conference of the Parties'. 2021 marked the 26th anniversary, thus giving it the title COP26.

in Glasgow even as I write these words. Such urgent questions must surely belong to world karma, rather than just our own individual destinies. So, I look forward to see if my guides will be able to enlighten us about such topical matters as these.

I have been aware of my closest spirit guides and of my ability to communicate with them telepathically for around 16 years. I shared some of these early conversations in my first book *Spirit Communications*, published in 2007. More recently, from 2016, I became aware of additional guides who were keen to contribute to a new book I intended to write. That book, entitled *Trusting in Spirit – The Challenge*, was published in 2018 and contained teachings from eight spirit guides. These included Philip, my own guardian angel, and the nature god, Pan. I had the clear impression that what I described as a 'circle of guides' formed around me to help with this particular project.

This was soon followed by another book, namely *Knowledge of Spirit Worlds and Life After Death* (2020), in which I asked my guides to give us insights into the nature of the spirit worlds *per se*, as well as of our post-death journeying.

Yet another project followed on from this, in which I asked the guides if they could map out an inner meditative pathway for us, in order to actually enter into the spirit worlds, thereby to gain our own first-hand personal experiences of these realms. This book, called *Journeying into Spirit Worlds, Safely and Consciously* was published in Spring 2022.

From the above, you will see that since 2016 I have been working actively with my guides on various research projects in the field of spirituality studies. In these enquiries I have made a point of giving a full account of how my communications with the guides come about. That is to say, the methodology employed. To make this transparent belongs to any good research. I emphasized how I needed to develop my trust and confidence in order to engage in this form of telepathic dialogue with the guides. Nonetheless, some people who have read my books may wonder if they express the fanciful outpourings of a sincere, but ultimately deluded, soul! I can sympathize with this sentiment, since I might perhaps have felt similarly sixteen years ago. However, my repeated experiences over these years have led me to the strong conviction that spirit guides do in fact exist, and that it is perfectly possible to converse with them. Moreover, two clairvoyant friends of mine were able independently to give confirmation of these particular guides.

As a student for 50 years of Rudolf Steiner's anthroposophy or spiritual science, I value a fully conscious relationship with spiritual beings and the worlds they inhabit. I have no interest in engaging in trance mediumship, hypnotic regression nor any psychic practices that might entail a lowering of self-consciousness. However, I do believe that a normal everyday consciousness can be, legitimately, expanded into a higher awareness of spirit realities. This is done through a spiritual training and discipline of our inner soul faculties. The fully conscious telepathic communications with my guides take place while I am still firmly grounded in earthly life. This is therefore a different situation to actually entering into the spirit worlds in order to meet such beings. I believe 'communication' is a more accessible possibility for many of us.

Now, the subject of this present book, 'karma in human life', is, I think, an important one, because it can help us to better understand the complexities of our lives on earth. When, for example, I walk through my local town and see other people milling back and forth, I wonder what destinies and challenges they each carry. What they carry has, I believe, been largely pre-planned before birth by their own inner spiritual being, though of course the majority of us have little or no inkling of this in our day-to-day selves. Therefore, we all go through our lives as best we can, dealing with whatever life throws at us. This may include some difficult relationships, sometimes with those closest to us. And there may be adverse circumstances to face in the form of illness or accidents, or other traumas. Fortunately, we also will have our share of joys and achievements to celebrate, which lighten our load on our earthly journeys.

I believe that all our experiences, both the good and bad, are there for us to learn from. If we can begin to understand how karma works, we will, I think, be able to make more sense of our various learning experiences. It is our own higher being who has set these opportunities for our own growth and development on our path of destiny. Therefore, in this book my intention is to ask my spirit guides to help us gain insights into the working of karma in our earthly lives.

I look forward to see what teachings they will give us, and how they will respond to the questions I will ask. As Joshua, my main guide, pointed out, I will need to be open to which guides wish to step forward and contribute. In undertaking such cooperative research, it is necessary to have an open and alert mind to what may be received.

I will not edit or change in any way what the guides bring through. Of course, I also do not know beforehand what this will be. Naturally, sceptics may say that I have surely assimilated many ideas to do with karma from my studies of Rudolf Steiner's teachings. Perhaps, therefore, what I imagine coming from the guides is nothing more than my own learned concepts. Reasonable though this speculation is, I do not think it is correct. When working with the guides, their thoughts flow through very fluently, without any effort on my own part. I think it unlikely that my own subconscious is involved in this process. Neither do I think that the guides are 'sub-personalities' of my psyche, as described in the psychosynthesis of Assagioli. No, my clear intention is to bring through accurately what the actual guides objectively are giving me.

So, having said this, we are nearly ready to turn to the theme of the second chapter, namely: what is karma? All the subsequent chapters and themes are also meant as questions, since they all belong in that same spirit of original research and enquiry. However, given the limitations of space, only certain subsequent additional questions can be included in the Q and A sessions following each of the teachings. Still, I hope the most pertinent ones will have been put and answered.

Let me then put this key question to Joshua:

Bob: Joshua, are the guides that I have worked with before ready and willing to engage with me on this project?

Joshua: Shalom, my friend. Yes, we are all willing to help you in every way that we can. Simply be open and receptive to whoever wishes to step forward first, in order to get this enquiry underway.

Bob: Right, Joshua, let us now see who will give us teachings on the fundamental nature of karma.

2.
WHAT IS KARMA?

Teachings

Raja Lampa: May I step forward to give the teachings on this theme of karma?

Bob: Please do so.

Raja: Yes, my friend. Let me say in the first place that the concept of karma is a very old one. It has been known for thousands of years in the East, and especially in India and Tibet. Although there has also been much recent interest in this term, it is often misunderstood, which leads to a false conception of what karma actually is. So, this really was the first thing that I wished to say.

Now, karma in its true form can rightly be called a 'law of life'. It is a law which unites all beings, not only on the earth but also in the heavens, so to speak. Karma is really a universal law and not simply an earthly one. This is the first thing to understand clearly. Karma is an all-pervasive and universal law which relates to all beings in the cosmos, whether living on earth or living in the stars. All beings, physical and spiritual, are held within the warm embrace of the law of karma. I say 'warm embrace' because it is a law which is filled with compassion. It is not a law which, with an iron grip, makes people or beings subservient to some almighty and dictatorial power. No, far from it. It is a law which is generated by love itself, and is there to bring order, recompense and compassion to all beings and their mutual relationships. Therefore, it is important to see all deliberations as to the workings of karma in this beneficent light. There is nothing cruel or harsh about karma. It is born out of love, and it is administered, so to speak, by beings of the highest levels of love and compassion.

So, my friend, this already begins to answer the question of what karma is. Exactly how it works in different circumstances and scenarios you will be exploring with my fellow guides in all the subsequent chapters. However, in this first incursion into this divine and holy law of life, it is necessary to give you the big picture, the universal picture.

Yes, karma regulates and orders the relationships between people living on the earth. This is true, and certainly, in order to understand human life better and deal with all of its challenges and surprises, a knowledge of the law of karma is very important. But remember, my friend, that to truly understand this law you cannot only rely simply on your clever intellect. This law is much greater and much deeper than what can be understood with the brain-based intellect. It also requires your heart. Your heart can have an understanding for things that goes much deeper than the head alone. You need to be able to feel and intuit the power of the law of karma working into the most subtle and delicate situations of life. It works in unseen ways, always seeking to bring about balance and healing. It is ultimately a healing law, a law which allows healing, balance and harmony to come about in all sentient beings. Therefore, it is truly *the* law that sustains the order and harmony of the universe.

Now, my friend, having said all this, you may still have in mind a characterization of karma that is often referred to, namely, 'as you sow, so you shall reap'. Now, this is very true, there is no denying it. But still, the law of karma embraces much more than just this. Yes, certainly, whatever you do in life has effects and consequences. Absolutely true. However, exactly how these consequences play out, exactly how they bring about a further course of events, does not just happen mechanically or mechanistically. No, life is far more complex than that! Much depends on how the effects are then dealt with by the beings who are acting upon the 'stage of life'. And this 'acting' takes account of free choice, of an ability to choose this path or that path.

This points to yet another misunderstanding about karma. It is often looked at in far too rigid a way, like some unalterable and unbending law, but it is not like that in reality. There are many ways in which karma can be met, and many ways in which it can unfold in order to help beings, including human beings, to learn the lessons which they need for their own progression. And this, my friend, is another essential aspect of karma. It enables learning and development to take place. It is not there as some system of punishment, as is so often wrongly conceived. No, it is there, fundamentally, as a learning experience so that people and beings can grow and become that which they already are in their essence.

So you see, my friend, that in answer to your question 'What is karma?' we have to look at various aspects which all belong to this living process. It is not a concept, at least not a dead concept, but a living reality, the reality of being. Beings stand behind karma. Beings have been given the task to administer karma out of love and wisdom. They have been given this task by the Creator Being of the cosmos – the being of Universal Love. So, when you think of karma, my friend, think of it as a gift from the Divine, a gift of love which will enable all beings to eventually find their true essence, their God-given identities. This, my friend, is what karma is about.

All blessings, Raja Lampa

Bob: Thank you.

Questions

Bob: Joshua, I have just read through the teachings which I received yesterday from Raja Lampa. I find that they are very clearly expressed. However, I would like to ask some questions about all this. Is this all right?

Joshua: Shalom, my friend. Yes, indeed, it is all right to ask questions, and we will see who of the guides wishes to come through to answer your queries.

Bob: Right. My first question is this: Karma is often described as a sort of spiritual law of 'cause and effect'. Namely, that some action is done in life and then, through karma, certain effects and consequences follow on. Is this correct?

Pierre: I would like to give you an answer to this particular question. Now, as Raja Lampa has already described to you, my friend, karma is more complicated and more all-encompassing than it is often conceived. So, although we understand when, as you say, it is described as a law of 'cause and effect', this should not be seen from

11

too narrow a viewpoint. Remember that karma can be enacted in a multitude of ways, not just one. It is not simply a linear connection between deeds. No, instead of that, it should be seen as capable of providing a variety of opportunities, in which the effects of a deed performed on earth can be met with and modulated in this or that manner. What we are trying to point out to you, my friend, is that it is not just a simple linear connection, as if a formula were being written to say that if A happens, then B automatically follows on from that. Rather, if A happens, then various letters of the alphabet may follow from that, not just B. In this way you begin to see, or sense, that karma is a living thing, a living law, and not a dead concept. As a living being, it can find numerous ways to express itself rather than being tied down or fixed in one direction only. We hope this answers your question.

Bob: Well, Pierre, it certainly makes the notion of 'cause and effect' into a much more versatile and mobile concept, shall I say, than might be first thought of. So, are you saying effectively that karma in its role of bringing balance and healing can be played out in a wide variety of ways? Is that what is meant?

Pierre: Yes, my friend, precisely so. It is a 'variable feast' rather than something that is rigidly fixed down and unbending. It can find expression in many different ways.

Bob: Right. But doesn't this sort of flexibility make it difficult to know just what consequences follow on from specific deeds and actions in life?

Joshua: Shalom, my friend. Let me step in here, please. As Pierre has pointed out, karma is much more complicated and creative than may at first be thought. It finds ways of working which will enable development and learning to take place according to the particular circumstances and situations in which human beings find themselves immersed. Because these things are complex, there are no hard and fast rules which apply to everyone in the same way. The beings who administer karma use their love and wisdom to guide the human beings on earth into directions that can bring about the greatest benefit for all concerned.

Bob: Well, how does this guidance from higher beings in spirit take account of human freedom then?

Joshua: Shalom, my friend. Freedom is taken account of in the sense that whatever guidance and directionality is given from above, it is still subject to the decision-making of the people who are involved. It does not interfere with this free decision-making, but rather supports it.

Bob: Yes, but what if a human being makes decisions which do not readily accept the workings of the law of karma?

Joshua: Well, in that case, the laws of karma will find different routes to accomplish what needs to be brought back into balance. Think of it like the many branches of a fast-flowing stream or river when it meets some obstacle in its path. It then flows around it in order to continue with its onward course. One branch goes this way, another that way. But whichever way is taken, the course of the river continues onwards.

Bob: Okay Joshua, I can see what you mean. However, wouldn't it be much easier to understand karma if this or that action produced a corresponding effect that could be easily described? I mean that a person has done something and therefore they must meet a particular effect or consequence?

13

Joshua: Yes, my friend, it is always much simpler to think of things happening in a clear-cut consequential fashion. However, as we said, karma has infinite possibilities within it. It is not tied down or fixed down to some immutable system of 'this' therefore 'that'.

Bob: Well, in that case, it will be very interesting to see what teachings are given in the chapters that follow, and which hopefully will increase our understanding of karma in human life.

Joshua: Yes, my friend. Let's see how the book develops.

All blessings, Joshua.

Bob: Joshua, there is actually still one more question I want to ask. Namely, karma is usually linked with reincarnation, in the sense that the laws of karma are seen as providing the connections and linkages between subsequent lives of individuals. Is this the case? And if so, can karma also work within the timeframe of the same lifetime as well? So really two questions here.

Joshua: Shalom, my friend. We will let Markos answer these questions for you.

Markos: Yes, my friend, it is good to be with you again. Now, in answer to these two questions, let me take them one at a time. First, yes, you're right to say that the law of karma is normally considered as the link between lifetimes. However, it not only applies to individuals, but also in a much wider sense to the karma of nations and races. However, we can leave the wider aspect for later teachings. So yes, karma is indeed forging links between the subsequent and also other lifetimes of individuals. As regards the second question, as to whether karma can also work within the one lifetime, the answer to this is: yes, it can. It can work from one stage of life in a person's development and learning to another. So, you see once again that it is important to understand the workings of karma in human life in a broad and inclusive way. It really affects all aspects of a person's time on earth, and also, to an extent, in the spirit worlds *per se*. Karma, as Raja Lampa has told you, is a universal law which encompasses all beings.

Bob: Thank you, Markos.

So, from the initial teachings given in this chapter, as a sort of base line, we will now branch out into the different themes of all the following ones.

3
KARMA IN RELATIONSHIPS

Bob: Joshua, I would like to receive the teachings for this third chapter. Who is willing to step forward for this?
Joshua Yes, Red Cloud is more than happy to work with you on this.
Bob: Right. Over to you, Red Cloud.

Teachings

Red Cloud: Thank you, my friend. Yes, it is again an honour to work with you, because we know that it is important that you do this work with us, in order to help enlighten those who seek clarity about such matters. So, the theme of 'karma in relationships' is, of course, a very wide one. As you know already, it is precisely in the realm of human relationships between people that karma is able to help bring about balance and harmony. Having said this, we do not pretend that this is always easy to achieve! In fact, it can sometimes be immensely difficult. You see, it is a matter of bringing together those people who often have real issues to resolve. People who have, more often than not, already been closely connected in their previous lifetimes with one another. In other words, there is often a long and deep history which connects people, even though, on the conscious everyday level, they are quite unaware of the connections which they already have. It is a matter then of people managing to come through to some sort of recognition that indeed they do have things to sort out with those particular people, be they family members, friends, or even enemies for that matter. And of course, it is much easier said than done. Very often, people do not wish to enter into confrontations or to be entirely honest with each other. Social conventions and fears about disturbing the status quo can prevent people from actually facing up to the issues which need to be resolved. So my friend, you can see, or begin to see, just how challenging and difficult it can be to balance karma, heal karma under such conditions. Nonetheless, karma is itself providing the opportunities for such resolutions to take place.

Karma is really a healing force or power that has the task, one can say, to bring about a new situation, a new balance of power. I say 'balance of power' because it is certainly possible to view relationships between people in terms of who is holding the power at any point in time. If only people would recognize this more consciously themselves, then this could facilitate a much quicker resolution of difficult – if not impossible – situations between them. Of course, this recognition would then need to be accompanied by a willingness to restore a more balanced and equitable situation for all who are involved. This can of course also be seen on the more macrocosmic level of balances of power between peoples and nations and of ethnic groupings within particular races. However, the bigger scenario can wait for a later chapter. In this chapter, our focus is on the relationships of individuals rather than groups.

So now, coming back to more particular situations, let me try to give you an example, or perhaps several examples. Let us say that, for instance, there is discord within a family between members of that family. It could be between husband and wife, father and mother, the children, etc. Various combinations are possible. However, the main point is that such people are not together arbitrarily. They have chosen to be together as part of that destiny situation. People are led together by their own volition within their prenatal* lives. Of course, when they find themselves in the earthly scenario, their wiser, spirit-based decisions to belong together in the blood-related family will not be remembered. But nonetheless, they have all contrived to bring about this close, familial contact for this lifetime. Why? Precisely because in their true higher beings, they have recognized they have things to work through and to sort out. This is nothing else but the working through of past karma. I say 'past karma' because, as you know, karma is also continually being created for the future. However, in the type of situation I have portrayed to you, of challenges within the family, this most often reflects past connections with those same people. How they then go about dealing with these challenges is left very much up to their own freedom, at least as adults. Clearly, the situation is rather different when children are involved, since they have still to develop their own personalities and maturity through life. But still, on whatever level the difficulties exist, one way or another karma and its laws will want to bring about a new balance and harmony between these individuals, whether children or adults.

---

*'Prenatal' here refers to one's life in the spiritual world before birth (or incarnation).

Now, my friend, a different example – not now in the family connections, but let's say someone that you meet who is able to give you a helping hand at a crucial or important time in your life. Here again, it is not arbitrary that you have met such a person. Rather, your destiny and karma have guided you together to find each other. You see here how kind karma is! It is a loving law that unites people who have links and who wish to be of support to each other in the circumstances of earthly life. It is truly a law of love. Yes, even in those circumstances when it leads, or appears to lead, to a conflict of interests, to difficult relations that have to be balanced somehow. But as I have said, it can also be experienced when extremely helpful and supportive relationships are made. In these ways, my friend, you can begin to see that there is actually a wise guidance taking place in life, and in people's lives. It is a guidance which also springs from their own higher natures as spirit beings, who stand behind the outer scenarios of earthly life. You are really spirit beings clothed in human bodies, not the other way around. I mean by this that you are essentially spirit beings, who then take on the human situation through incarnating into human bodies and developing through the course of human life through growing up.

As you will realize, my friend, there are countless ways in which karma works in human relationships. Just as each person's life and biography is unique to them, so the ramifications and manifestations of karma are infinite, we can say. There are millions, billions, of human souls living on earth at any one time (even though this was not always the case) and so there are billions of ways in which karma is being enacted and manifested in their earthly lives. Therefore, with this realization I will bring my teachings to a close and invite you, my friend, to put your questions to me and the other guides.

All blessings, Red Cloud

Bob: Thank you.

Questions

Bob: Right, Joshua, having read through the teachings from Red Cloud, I will now ask some questions and see who will step forward to answer them. How do we recognize 'past karma' from 'future' in human relationships? Is there a way of differentiating these two streams, so to speak?

Markos: Let me try to answer this question, please. Now, how to differentiate what belongs to the past and what leads into the future is in many ways not easy to do. However, generally we can say that past karma is shown when people are born into various situations in life and have various people around them. Obviously, this will be family members in the first place, the people, the individuals with which you find your place in life. You grow up in a particular family setting and you have connections, links, also with the wider family which goes beyond your immediate parents, siblings, etc. So, with these people you obviously have a connection from the very beginning of your new life on earth. These connections are mainly, if not entirely, due to past karmic relationships. So, this on the one hand. However, as you grow up through childhood and adolescence and into adulthood, not only does your own personality develop, but you also meet other people who have an influence on your life. These can be teachers, friends, perhaps other relations, and also complete strangers who suddenly appear within the circumference of your life. Now, the sort of relationships which you form with these people can lead, and does lead, to the development of fresh, new karma, which leads into the future. In other words, it is not just a question of sorting out past karma and healing it, but of charting new lines of direction which lead you into future scenarios and which bring about new decisions and actions. These in turn form the karma which, in a later life, will constitute past karma for you to fulfil. So you can see, my friend, that the question of past and future karma is a continual process of becoming, of creating, of working with the living forces of life which unites you with other individuals. It is a kaleidoscopic play of interweaving forces which guide you through this way or that, in order to help you to achieve the aims and goals which you have set for yourselves. It is not willy-nilly, so to speak. It is, in fact, extremely meaningful and provides the fabric, the weft and weave, of your own destiny course.

Bob: Thank you, Markos. I think I understand what you are pointing to with this. Another question. Sometimes people really appear to tie themselves up in knots with others. I mean, get tied up in relationships that appear even destructive, and lead to a lot of unhappiness – maybe also repeating cycles of behaviours that just get them deeper and deeper into despair. Why is this?

21

Raja Lampa: My friend, let me step forward for this. Yes, you are right that sometimes in life people really do get ensnared into the most oppressive and restrictive relationships with others. This happens when people give up their own power to others in an unhealthy way. Often it is due to lack of confidence in themselves and a consequent need to feel supported and carried along by others. This then easily leads to an abusive type of relationship, because the weaker person becomes so terribly dependent on the so-called stronger personality. Actually, both are weak, but it shows in different ways. Now, is this a 'karmic situation' in which they find themselves? Yes, it may well be, but it is by no means healthy! Rather, we would say that karma has brought this about in order to give them the opportunity to grow beyond this subservience; to grow stronger precisely by being immersed and embroiled in this negative situation. You see, my friend, it is by having to deal with and overcome such difficult and unhappy circumstances that people can find themselves in a new way – provided, that is, that they resolve to step out of the restrictive and constricted situation they are presently in. Once they, or at least one of them, breaks out from this destructive cycle of events, then a new pathway opens up for them and they discover themselves anew.

Bob: Yes, Raja, I see what you mean by this. It seems to me that karma works in all manner of complicated situations of life. Not so?

Raja: Yes, indeed it does, and therefore it is really a matter of seeing how that is with each person at each point in their lives. On the other hand, my friend, as you know from your own experience, when you are able to look back over life, you can more easily see the links and connections with the people you have met and encountered on your journey. In retrospect, it becomes easier to see the direction you are travelling in and how various people were there to help you on your path. Not so?

Bob: Yes, that has certainly been my experience, though at the time it was not possible to actually see how one thing would lead to another.

Raja: Yes, that is so. Life has to be lived, and through the living, the way forward is gradually, or eventually, revealed.

Bob: Yes, that is true, at least in my experience, and I can imagine that this also applies to others on their own journeys.

Joshua: Perhaps at this point you wish to bring this chapter to an end? We will be exploring many aspects of karma and its workings in the chapters to come.

Bob: Yes, Joshua, I think this is a good idea. Thank you.

4
KARMA IN ILLNESS

Bob: Joshua, with this chapter I would like to receive teachings concerning karma in illness as it affects human life. Are you and the other guides willing to cooperate with me in this today?

Joshua: Shalom, my friend. Yes, we are. Let us see who wishes to step forward to give the teachings today.

Teachings

Gopi Ananda: Yes, I will give the teachings today, thank you. So, let me say to begin with that the question of how illnesses work with karma in human life is a very important matter. Important because there are many perplexities, shall I say, when it comes to trying to understand the impact which illnesses of all different sorts have on the lives of human beings.

Illnesses, as you know, take many different forms. However, it is a karmic fact that through illness it is possible to bring about healing in human life. Now, straightaway this sounds like a contradiction in terms. How can we possibly equate illness with healing? After all, it is in illness that we seek for healing to overcome the illness, whatever form it happens to take. However, this is not really a contradiction, because it is just through experiencing the condition of illness that the possibilities for karmic healing can unfold. We are here speaking about the healing of karmic situations and karmic consequences, often accruing from past misdemeanours, we can say, provided we do not view this too judgementally. That is to say that such misdemeanours are enacted through ignorance of their effects in the longer term. Only if we are able to perceive the longer-term effects of our actions, can we take the best course of action for all concerned. And as I have said, this requires a wide enough perspective of the particular situations in which we are placed, again by karma. The workings of karma are complicated and complex. They are not simple, and it is a mistake to try to simplify these complex questions into purely 'cause and effect' roles, in too simple a way. Often, there are rather convoluted and intricate twists of fate and destiny which need to happen in order that the laws of karma can work effectively. That is, to work in such a way that a true balance and harmony can come about.

Now, my friend, I can already discern that you will have many questions which belong to this theme, and it will be important that you can put these questions to us. As I have said, illness in its many forms makes a significant and often profound impact on the course of human lives. Therefore, it is only in looking at specific situations, with the particular individuals involved in these situations, that a more concrete explanation can be given as to 'why' that particular illness needed to be experienced at just that moment in that person's life. And of course, the illness does not only affect the person who suffers it, but many more people are touched by it also: family, friends, relatives, doctors, nurses, etc. A wider circle of people become involved with that illness situation, and therefore its impact spreads out to others, like the ripples spreading out on a pond when a stone is thrown into it. So you see, my friend, that much is entailed when we turn to this question of karma and illness. However, fundamentally speaking, illnesses occur in order to balance karma for the individuals involved, and for the wider group of people who are involved to a greater or lesser extent. The laws of love have given illness as the means for a new balance, a new orientation, a new possibility, for forward development to take place. Therefore, strange as it may seem, illness should really be looked at as a gift, a blessing in many ways, because it alone can provide the means for new and important steps to be made in the lives of individuals. Yes, illness is often looked upon as a curse rather than a blessing, but this is because it is seen from too narrow a perspective, and not with the benefit of a wider circumference. This width can only be obtained by seeing how the linkages work, from earthly life to earthly life. Only on the background of a real understanding of reincarnation and repeated earthly incarnations, can the karmic effects of illnesses be seen in the clearest light. So, to sum up, my friend, illness is to be seen as a gift of the gods, to enable human beings to evolve and develop towards their true recognition as spirit beings – spirit-beings who are members of a divine order, and not simply earthly beings. This is the wider meaning of illness in relationship to the workings of karma.

All blessings, Gopi Ananda

Bob: Thank you.

Questions

Bob: Joshua, can I now ask some questions concerning this important theme?

Joshua: Shalom, my friend. Yes, please do ask whatever questions you have, and we will endeavour to answer them.

Bob: Right. Actually, there are so many possible questions on this matter that it is difficult to know where to begin. However, let me start with this. I have recently, within the past two years, lost two good friends of mine to cancer. There will be many people who have had similar experiences with this particular pernicious illness. How do such circumstances relate to karma?

Markos: I would like to answer this question, please. Now, in the first place, let me say that this is not an easy matter to discuss. It is not easy because we are all too aware of how devastating this illness, cancer, can be on the course of human life, and how many people this affects. It is truly an illness of your time. However, just for that reason, it also has a particular role to play in the working through of karma. You see, it is not for nothing that certain illnesses are rife and widespread in a particular period of time – historical time, I mean. Cancer is a modern illness; it is not an illness which was to be found in, for example, the so-called Middle Ages, nor in more 'primitive' – and in that sense, 'natural' – situations of life, for example with indigenous races, etc. No, it is very much a modern scourge. However, it does have an important role to play in helping to balance out karmic situations from the past, and also those which lead on into the future.

Having said all this, we know what hardship and sorrow is caused when this illness strikes a person down – when either through the course of the illness itself, or even through the effects of the sorts of treatment used to alleviate it, a person's health deteriorates more and more. This often leads to a so-called 'premature death'. Karma nonetheless works its way through just these difficult situations. Look at it like this. Ask yourself objectively what can a person learn from going through this illness, even if it eventually leads to his or her death? It is possible to learn things from this that cannot be learnt otherwise. It is, in effect, a difficult, even drastic, opportunity to learn lessons which cannot be provided through the ordinary course of life. It is precisely through this learning, on all levels of the soul, that the person, the ill person, can make personal, individual progress. This is the great enigma of such situations of illness. On the one hand, they are thoroughly debilitating, and on the other hand, they are actually the medicine that is required for true karmic healing to take place! It is only when it is really possible to overview and overlook the course of a person's repeated lives on earth that the 'whys and wherefores' of this situation can be thoroughly grasped and recognized. So this, my friend, is the answer, the rather long answer, which I have given to your heartfelt question.

Bob: Thank you, Markos. Clearly, cancer is a prevalent illness in our time, and therefore provides a stark example. However, there are probably hundreds if not thousands of illnesses to which human beings can be subject. These range from the common cold to various chronic and acute forms of illness that may disable people or even be life-threatening. They affect not only adults but also children, and even infants and babies. So overall, illness in all its many forms is part and parcel of human life on earth. There is no escaping it, is there?

Pierre: No, there isn't. As you rightly say, it is something that affects everyone on earth in one way or another. No one, or hardly anyone, is going to be free of illness in the course of their life. However, there is clearly a big difference between relatively minor illnesses and those which have a major impact on the quality of a person's life. There is, therefore, a very wide spectrum indeed, and it is only possible to speak in generalities unless we would take a particular example, either of a particular illness, or how it affects a particular person or a group of people.

Bob: So, what's best to gain an understanding of karma in illnesses? What do you suggest?

Pierre: Well, my friend, we are really looking at the bigger picture. The bigger picture shows how illnesses, major or minor, are enabling karmic balance and karmic recompense to take place, whether for individuals or larger groups of people. In all such cases, karma makes good use of what the illness can offer. I realize this may seem a strange way of putting it, but nonetheless, it really is the case that karma works through the illnesses as a way of bringing about balance and health! This is looking at health not just of the physical body, as the instrument of the soul and spirit, but also on the deeper levels of a person's make-up. As you know, a person consists of a number of 'bodies', we can say. These are sometimes called the etheric body, the astral body, and so on. There are also spirit bodies *per se*. So, true health requires that all members – or bodies – of a person are in balance with each other, that there is harmony and not discord. It is in establishing, or trying to establish, this balance that illnesses have their role to play. Illness is really the chief means to restore karmic balance and to restore karmic health in its widest perspective. This, you could say, is the mission or task of illness as such. So this, my friend, *is* the bigger picture, and it is within this bigger picture that all the many types, forms, species, of illnesses have to be seen. That is, karmically speaking.

Bob: Thank you for now.

*

Bob: Joshua, I would like to take up again the theme of yesterday, and pose further questions re. illness and karma. Is that all right?

Joshua: Shalom, my friend. Yes, it is. Do ask your questions and we will see who steps forward to answer them.

Bob: Right. The first question today is this: 'How do we know whether, when a person becomes ill, that *that* illness is karmic?' I'm assuming that not *all* illnesses that a person may have in his or her life have necessarily a karmic origin, nor a karmic recompense in the future. Am I right in this?

Raja: Well, my friend, you ask here two important questions, which I will attempt to answer for you. Let us take the second of your questions first, namely, whether all illnesses are karmic in relation to past or future events. No, they are not, at least not in the sense that a person has become ill because of some past events in a former life, say, nor that they are ill in order to learn a lesson for their future life. Although it is true to say that all experiences, and therefore all illnesses, can be seen as learning opportunities, nonetheless we cannot say that all illnesses are karmic. What we can say is that when an illness has a major impact on a person's life, and probably those who are close to that person, then, in all likelihood, the illness has a karmic significance, both for the balancing of past deeds and the consequences for future ones.

So, it needs to be seen, in each case, just how important or significant the condition of illness is in that person's biography, how life-changing it may be. This is the clearest indication of the workings of karma into that particular situation. So, with that answer, my friend, I think we have actually addressed both your questions. To summarize: not all illnesses are karmic, but those that are will have a significant impact on the course of that person's life.

Bob: Thank you, Raja. It appears to me, from what you and the other guides have said, that it will only be by considering a particular case, that is a particular person, and following events through, that the karmic significance and reasons will be made plain, or at least be clearer. Not so?

Raja: Precisely, my friend. While it is useful to speak in generalities in order to gain an understanding of the big picture, it is only by focusing on particular cases that a deeper understanding of the reasons for that illness will be made clear. But this, of course, requires more esoteric research, we could say.

Bob: Yes, but is it not perhaps possible to point karmically to the characteristics of certain illnesses and their origins in past incarnations? For example, let's say, pneumonia or heart disease, compared to multiple sclerosis or other chronic conditions? In other words, can we karmically trace a particular illness to a quite particular karma? Yes, that is the question.

Raja: Well, to some extent we can do this. So, let us say an illness that affects the lungs may be traced back to a particular form of sexuality in a previous life, or a condition of multiple sclerosis may be traced back to a certain narrow-mindedness in a previous incarnation, and so on. This is possible to do. However, even with this, we have to take into account the individualization of these qualities or characteristics, such that they can be different for each individual, each entelechy. So you see, karma is really very complicated because you can't simply pin it down and say that B follows A, no matter what. Because karma is based on love, it looks carefully at each person's position, at every stage of their life and lifetimes. It is individualized in a loving and compassionate way.

Bob: Well, then it seems to me that perhaps the most important message coming out of this chapter is that illness is meaningful, and ultimately helpful for the development and progress of each person. Is that right?

Joshua: Yes, my friend, this is correct, and this gives the best possible attitude towards dealing with illness. To see, or sense, that it is certainly not for nothing, especially so when it has a major impact on that individual's life.

Bob: I think one obvious question that follows on from all of this is: 'Should we do all we can to heal or cure illnesses, even if we believe they have karmic purpose and meaning?'

Red Cloud: Yes, we should do everything possible to find cures for illnesses. However, we should try to see that the means of curing does not do more harm than the illness itself! By this I mean that while it is perfectly legitimate

32

and moral to do all we can to help a person come through, or bear, their illness, we should also endeavour not to make matters worse, in terms of suffering, by our interventions. In other words, a truly humane and empathetic approach must be applied, with a sensitivity to how that person is responding to whatever measures we take. This requires really listening to how the person is managing to live through his/her condition. If the right approach is found, then this may well succeed in overcoming the illness in a truly beneficial way for that person.

Bob: So, illnesses can be healed in such a way that karma is also fulfilled?

Joshua: Yes, it can. This then constitutes a true healing process for that person, karmically as well as physically, shall we say.

Bob: Well of course, there are not only so-called physical illnesses but also, nowadays, people are becoming much more conscious of forms of mental illness, including emotional problems, etc. Again, do the latter also have karmic roots and consequences?

Raja: They can do, but not necessarily. Again, it is a question that can only be answered in the individual case, and by doing the necessary research.

Bob: Very well, thank you. It has become clear in this chapter that illness is an important way, or process, in which karmic balance can be brought about. True?

Raja: Very true, and this is why illness is to be found on the earthly plane.

All blessings, Raja

Bob: Thank you.

5
KARMA IN THE PANDEMIC

Bob: Joshua, two years on since I wrote Chapter 4, 'Karma in Illness', the whole of humanity is now living with the effects of the global coronavirus pandemic. This is an ongoing problem, as new variants of the virus appear. Whilst medical science has succeeded in producing various vaccines to protect people from the worst effects of the illness, the new variants might defy these measures. At any event, I think I must ask if we can view the pandemic karmically. That is to say, could there be any karmic reasons why it has happened to humanity at this particular time? I'm not sure, Joshua, how you and the other guides would like to address this theme. Do you want to give us new teachings followed by questions, or would you prefer to go straight into the questions I will ask? How best to proceed?

Joshua: Shalom, my friend. Let us give you some teachings first, and then you can follow them up with your own questions.

Bob: Right, Joshua, I will see who wants to come through for this.

Red Cloud: Yes, I will give you some teachings.

Bob: Thank you.

Teachings

Red Cloud: Let me say to begin with that so-called pandemics, whenever they occur and affect a large number of people, are there for a reason. They are not arbitrary. So, the question then is, for what reason has a particular pandemic afflicted human beings on earth? Let us explore this in relation to the particular pandemic which you are all dealing with right now.

The reason for its manifestation has to be seen in the wider background of humanity's relationship to the other kingdoms of nature, and in particular to the animal kingdom. You see, my friend, the animals have suffered a great deal at the hands of humanity. A great deal of pain and suffering has been caused, and often deliberately, to the animal kingdom – to, if I may express it so, your brothers and sisters in evolution. Yes, you may find this a strange way to express it, but bear in mind that in my last incarnation, among the Sioux Nation,* we had a very deep and intimate connection to nature, and to the animals especially. We depended entirely upon the animals that lived in our land, for our livelihood and our welfare. Therefore, although we hunted the animals for food and clothing, etc., nonetheless, we also had deep respect for their being and existence.

In your modern times, this respect and devotion is no longer there. Yes, there is a certain amount of sentimentality towards certain of your domesticated animals, and those you keep as pets, but this is very different to the deep respect which I am referring to.

---

*Native American tribe.

35

So this, my friend, has to do with the background, the reason we can say why this particular pandemic has afflicted you all. It is because you have usurped a [particular] relationship with the animals that the conditions for this pandemic have arisen.

Only by bringing about a different relationship, a more humane and dignified relationship, will you address the root causes of this widespread disease. Now, my friend, this should already point the way for you to be able to understand the pandemic in terms of karma, in this case what we can call 'world karma'. You see, my friend, only when you wake up to your responsibilities as custodians of the earth and of the various kingdoms of nature will you be able to effect the right balance and harmony for all life forms. This pandemic therefore has a deeper meaning – yes, a karmic meaning – for the whole of the human race. And the meaning is clear enough, if only more people would open themselves to receive it: namely, to restore the damaged connection, the damaged relationship, which you have with the natural world and with your fellow lifeforms and species on planet earth. This is the deeper karmic reason behind the current pandemic. If this is taken seriously and addressed, then a true healing can take place. And this is what the law of karma, the law of love, is asking of humanity. Learn to treat nature and all its kingdoms as your friends, not your enemies. Then healing help will follow on, because nature in herself is always ready to forgive, so to speak, always ready to make recompense for the harm that has been done to her. It lies within the responsibility of human beings to heal their own illnesses, their own karmic consequences, by changing their attitudes and viewpoints. A complete change of attitude is required if a true and lasting healing is to be effected. Vaccinations may soften the immediate impact of the illness, but the deeper causes also need to be addressed. Otherwise, you may be sure that one pandemic will be followed by another and another. Lessons need to be learned if this scourge is to be lifted from the shoulders of mankind. But *you* need to do the lifting!

All blessings, Red Cloud

Bob: Thank you, Red Cloud. I will come back with questions when I have had time to digest what you said.
Red Cloud: Yes, we will look forward to that.

Questions

Bob: So, Red Cloud, I'm not sure whether you or another guide will answer my questions. Can you let me know this?
Red Cloud: Yes, my friend, Isobel would like to step forward now to answer your questions on this theme.
Bob: Right, thank you. Isobel, there are probably many questions to ask, since we are still plunged within this pandemic, and may be for years to come. So, the first question is: Did this pandemic begin or have its origins in the Wuhan wet market in China, as many people believe, or not?
Isobel: Well, my friend, this is indeed an interesting question. You only have to ask yourself, in the light of Red

Cloud's teachings, how are the animals being treated in such markets? Are they treated with respect and kindness, or rather are they being abused and mistreated? I think the answer should be obvious to you all. Therefore, with this you also have the answer you seek. The breeding ground for the present pandemic happened in this very situation. However, my friend, we can also say that this was the 'touchstone', so to speak. As Red Cloud has already explained clearly, the wrong relationship between humanity and the whole animal kingdom was at the root of the problem. Therefore, only by addressing this root problem will a real answer be found to overcoming or eradicating the disease, the virus.

Bob: Thank you, all that makes sense to me. But looking at all this now in terms of karma, can you say more about it? What it means, say, for our future as a race?

Isobel: Well, my friend, this is a big question, is it not? Let us first consider what has led you all into the situation. Namely, the usurping of your power over the animal kingdom. By not treating these fellow creatures, be they big or small, with the respect that they deserve, you yourselves have created this harmful situation – for yourselves! Yes, you are the conductors of your own fate, so to speak. Therefore, there are lessons to be learnt.

If these lessons are learnt, if there is a real change of heart on the part of human beings, then some good can come of all this. You see, my friend, already the effects of the pandemic have caused many people to look at their life differently. Just remember what happened when you had, in different parts of the world, your so-called 'lockdowns'. That is to say, when normal life came to a halt. When, for example, the sky was free from planes and their vapour trails. Or when you could breathe air that was cleaner because the cars were off the roads. Or, when you could go out into nature and appreciate it with fresh eyes. There were, were there not, many advantages to losing, for a time, your normal, habitual ways of life?

If, in addition to this, some people at least began to think more deeply about their lives and its meaning, then you have the possibility of a quite new point of view to arise. Perhaps even a more spiritual, existential point of view. So you see that this pandemic can have real advantages for you, and not simply drawbacks.

Bob: Yes, Isobel, I have often thought along just those lines. But on the other hand, the pandemic also brought about a tremendous amount of fear in people, didn't it?

Isobel: It did indeed. But even this, if it leads to some sort of awakening, can be turned to good, almost like a shock therapy, you could say.

Bob: Well, it's certainly true that many people have suffered great shocks, especially if close loved ones have died prematurely in this pandemic. These shocks may well have been almost too much to bear. Can any good come out of that?

Isobel: Well, my friend, there you have to look carefully at each case – at each particular situation and the people who are involved. But remember, we are here dealing with an event of world karma. We have to look at the bigger picture, even though it is true that its impact is felt also at a very personal and individual level.

Bob: So, in terms of 'world karma', what does all this mean for our futures?

Isobel: It means that if the lessons are learnt, in the sense of recognizing the underlying causes, then real and substantial changes for the better, for the good of all, will follow. Never have you lived at a more crucial time for world history, in the sense that what will come to pass really does depend upon human will – that is, free will. If people resolve to change that which is rotten in their attitudes and behaviours – and that includes all those in positions of power – then something very good will come about. Good karma, one can say, will be created. And this good karma will be to the benefit of everyone who lives on the earth, including the animals and other forms of life. But, as Red Cloud has said already, it does depend on human beings truly becoming custodians of the earth, really in a sacred sense – a sense in which all life is valued and appreciated properly. Only if this happens can there be a truly good future for humanity. And in this sense, everything does lie in your own hands. This is no trite saying, but a reality, and the sooner it is taken seriously, deadly seriously, the better it will be.

Bob: Yes, I can believe this. So, what you're saying, Isobel, is that we all can create the future through our deeds and our motivations and behaviours. Is that right?

Isobel: That's absolutely right, and never was there a time when this realization was more important than now.

Bob: Can the current virus then be actually overcome, annihilated, so to speak?

Isobel: It can, if there are the right conditions for this to happen. Remember, my friend, that behind all things there are really spirit beings of one sort or another. The same applies to viruses. Beings stand behind them. The so-called virus is but a manifestation of the activity of certain beings, spiritually speaking. These activities can cease, will cease, when they are no longer fed and nurtured by the attitudes which allowed them to come about in the first place. Just as a being on earth will die if its food is cut off, so these virus-beings will die if they are no longer fed. In this way, it is true to say that the cause of the pandemic can be overcome.

Bob: So, what is the most important attitude or attribute to conquer the virus?

Isobel: It is love. Love will conquer all ills, provided it is a true and unselfish love. This, fundamentally, is also what the law of karma is: a 'law of love' designed to bring about the greatest good.

Bob: Thank you. I think this is the right note to end on.

Postscript

In the UK government-sponsored vaccine promotions that are shown on television and in newspapers, vaccinated people have a thin layer of light all around their bodies, almost like a kind of stylised auric field. Just think how much more potent and powerful that would actually be if it was a strong aura of pure love for all life on earth! This, however, would have to be created through sincere individual effort and altruism, not by having – however many – jabs! It would be that love which does indeed hold sacred all life on planet earth.

6
KARMA IN ACCIDENTS

Bob: Joshua, I'd like to begin this theme today. I wonder who wishes to give the teachings?
Joshua: Shalom, my friend. Yes, Red Cloud would like to do this today.
Bob: Right.

Teachings

Red Cloud: Háu, my friend. Yes, I would like to give you teachings on this important theme, which is rather different from the theme of the previous chapters. It is one thing to suffer illness and it is another thing to suffer an accident. Why? Because the circumstances are different. It is the very nature of accidents that they come to us 'out of the blue', so to speak. They are completely unexpected. Whereas in the case of illness, there can be, and usually are, very clear signs that all is not well. In the case of accidents, it can hit us suddenly, like a bombshell. So, this is the first thing that needed to be pointed out – that accidents lead us into a quite different sort of scenario than illnesses.

Of course, I'm speaking in general terms, because, as is necessary in each of the chapters, we need to try to give you the big overall picture in the first place. When you then ask us questions, we can try to be a little more specific, shall we say. So, let us proceed.

Accidents by their very nature happen to us when we least expect them. Accordingly, we are usually, if not always, quite unprepared for what then takes place. We can be shocked, traumatized, surprised and scared by what befalls us. We wonder, 'Why has this happened to me?' or '...to us?' if it involves more people than just yourself. We then try to understand and make sense of the new situation in which we find ourselves.

Now of course, there are accidents and accidents. By this I mean that some accidents are quite small and minor affairs that do not have profound effects upon our lives. On the other hand, some accidents are very major affairs and can completely change our lives in ways that we had not imagined before. Now, with these latter accidents, we can readily perceive, or sense, shall I say, the workings of karma. And remember, we are considering this theme in the light of karma, trying to understand better how karma can work through the events in our lives. So, whenever we see that a really significant impact has been made on our previously 'normal' way of life, we can be pretty sure that karma is working and trying to teach us something important. Yes, my friend, it is quite good, perhaps very good, to see karma as your teacher, as the one who comes to you, in order to help you to realize something about yourself, or your relationship with others. Karma is in many ways like a good friend who says to you: 'Please wake up and see what needs to happen in your life if you're to make progress and not just carry on in the same old way.' And it is just here, with such learning and development opportunities, that so-called accidents have an important role to play. I say 'so-called accidents' deliberately, because even though you may not realize it, nine times out of ten you yourself have orchestrated the accident that befalls you. Not, of course, with your normal, everyday consciousness, but rather out of your higher consciousness. I mean, that consciousness which you always have in your inner being, your spirit being.

As a spirit being, you know already what you want to achieve with your present earthly life. You know already what are the goals and aims which you set before yourself when you entered into this new incarnation. So-called accidents are events which *you* have brought about at certain moments in your life, in order to make a new step forward. This step forward belongs to the karma which you carry within you. It is something which helps to determine your course – or path – in life. Now, when I say 'determine', this is not to be understood as some sort of blind fate. There is nothing blind about it. You yourself have foreseen what needs to come about in order for you to receive that jolt, we could say – that shock which enables you to make a new step forward in your own development.

So, my friend, with this we are giving you a way to view accidents not as 'accidents' are usually understood, but as karmic events that are ultimately to your benefit, even though at the time you may think them to be the opposite. This is the important teaching on karma in accidents which we wished to give you today.

All blessings, Red Cloud

Bob: Thank you.

Questions

Bob: So, Joshua, I will now ask questions on this theme. I wonder who will step forward from the guides? The first question is this: The notion that we ourselves bring about accidents deliberately in our lives will seem very strange to many people, won't it?

Markos: Yes, my friend, it will certainly sound very strange to many people, as you say. Nevertheless, most so-called accidents are actually brought about by yourselves. In other words, they are not simply chance events. No, they happen for a reason, and as Red Cloud pointed out, when these accidents have an incisive effect on your lives, they are more likely than not an expression of the workings of karma. This is an important way in which karma comes through into ordinary daily life and says to you: 'Something needs to change, something new needs to happen for you to progress in your own development.' It is precisely through the accident that this change can be facilitated.

Bob: Well, Markos, I can see that this is certainly a way in which karma can work, but accidents can be pretty awful things. Let's say, for example, a serious car crash that can cause serious injuries.

Markos: Yes, you are correct in saying that. However, although it is the last thing which a person wanted to happen in their life from their ordinary point of view, it is just the thing that needed to happen from a higher viewpoint!

Bob: Okay, but it could really be quite devastating and be the cause of much sorrow and hardship, couldn't it?

Markos: Yes, it could indeed, but unfortunately – or fortunately – depending on your viewpoint, it is nonetheless something that serves to completely change the status quo. It brings new possibilities into that person's, or those people's, lives.

Bob: Would such a serious accident somehow be related to a person's karma, originating out of past events, say in a former life, or could it be creating new karma for the future, perhaps for the next incarnation?

Pierre: It can be both of these. In a sense, it will be both, because there is a continuous chain of events linking past and future. So, in that sense, it has to be seen as embedded in an ongoing stream, rather like a sudden obstacle occurring in a fast-flowing stream. The water continues, but its course is altered, to an extent at least, by the obstacle or intrusion which has entered in. It becomes a changed situation.

Bob: And is this changed situation always for the good of that person, and for others who may be involved or affected by it? Does it always lead to good, positive results?

Pierre: Yes, in the end it will, even though the immediate aftermath may seem pretty negative and even destructive. Nonetheless, karmically speaking, it will be used for the greatest good of those involved. If karma has brought this about, then it has done so in order that new steps can be made on the forward path.

Bob: Well, you say *if* karma has brought this about... This implies that karma *per se* may not have done so. Does this mean that some accidents really are totally new, unplanned-for events that break into a person's life?

Pierre: Yes, this can be the case. In other words, that there is nothing from the past, from the time leading up to the event, which has in any way necessitated this particular accident.

Bob: So, it is truly an 'accident', in the way most people would think of it, right?

Pierre: Yes, it is, but nonetheless, because it has occurred, it will of necessity have karmic implications for that person's future life.

Bob: Yes, that is clear. Let me ask another question. Sometimes we meet or encounter another person as it were 'by accident'. In other words, this person, perhaps a stranger, is not someone we ever expected to meet, is not one of our known friends or acquaintances. However, this accidental meeting may make a great difference to our future life. Is this a karmic event? Has karma brought this person to us, or us to him or her?

Markos: Yes, absolutely. This is a very good example of where karma steps in and leads us in a new direction. Yes, that stranger may well have been one of our closest companions in a former lifetime, and now in this life steps forward at just the right time to lead us on.

Bob: So, once again, has this been orchestrated or arranged by ourselves?

Markos: Fundamentally, this is the case. It is something that we have built into our own life-plan for this incarnation.

Bob: So, we all have such a life-plan, a blueprint perhaps, for our forthcoming life?

Markos: Yes, we do. Every person plans what they want to achieve in their earthly life, so that they can make progress on their spiritual journey. Remember, my friend, that ultimately everyone is on a journey to find themselves, and to do this, a definite course of action is planned for each new lifetime.

Bob: So, nothing is left to chance? Nothing is arbitrary?

Markos: No, it isn't. Everything has meaning and purpose, even if it seems to be well camouflaged in everyday life.

Bob: Well, to know this, I think, would be reassuring for most of us.

Markos: Yes, it should be, because it shows that each human life is imbued with value and purpose. Nothing is wasted, but everything has its part to play in the greater scheme of things.

Bob: So, I think with this good thought, I will bring this chapter to a close. Thank you everyone.

7
KARMA IN EVOLUTION

Bob: Dear Joshua, I would like this morning to see who would like to give teaching on this theme of 'karma in evolution'. Is that all right?

Joshua: Shalom, my friend. Yes, it is all right, and actually Philip, your guardian angel, wishes to give teaching on this theme.

Bob: Right, in that case, over to you, Philip.

Teachings

Philip: My friend and brother, I am happy to be able to come through to you with teachings on this particular subject, which is, of course, a very broad one. It really does encompass the whole course of 'world evolution', so to speak, or even better put, cosmic evolution, because karma is not just something that belongs to the earth realm. No, it extends much further than that. It reaches into all corners of the universe, so to speak. Therefore, it is truly a universal law, a law of love that embraces all beings on all levels.

Now, in what way can we understand this, my friend and brother? You see, it is a law, a way of life, we can say, that has been put in place by the Creator Being of the cosmos. It is therefore inbuilt into the very substance of the universe, which includes the spirit worlds as well as the earthly plane of existence. Now, you may well be surprised by this. If you have thought of karma as fundamentally a law which only affects human beings, then it can be surprising to realize that all beings are subject to the same law. That is to say, it also applies to the angels, of whose ranks I am a member, to the archangels and to all the company of heaven.

You ask: 'But how can this apply to spirit beings?' It is obvious, we can say, how this applies to human beings and their deeds, but it is not at all obvious how this works with higher beings. Are they not exempt from this? And the answer is no, they/we are not. All beings, whatever their rank or position, have to abide by the laws of karma, because it is these laws which ensure that a just and ethical situation is reached on all levels. But you might say: 'Surely spirit beings would not do things to usurp the order or harmony of the universe?' Well, my friend, there are indeed some spiritual beings who do their very best to do precisely that! Beings who have fallen behind the course of normal progression and evolution for their kind, for their level of development. In other words, my friend and brother, all is not perfect in heaven, as it is also not perfect on earth. No, there are challenges to be met on all levels of being. Therefore, the law of karma is both relevant and necessary in order to restore balance and harmony. If any beings have transgressed the proper mode of behaviour, so to speak, then there must be recompense and restoration of their deeds, so as to bring back the necessary balance of power. Yes, it is 'the balance of power', however strange it may seem to you that I use such words. You see, deeds matter on each and every level.

This is something which you fully recognize applying to the earthly levels of being. You know full well that what a person does is consequent in its effects in a wider sense. It does not just rest there, in limbo, so to speak. No, ripples spread out from the actions that are done, and affect others. Something is set in motion, just as when dropping a stone into water, and this spreads outwards to have a much wider effect than might be imagined at first. So you see, in this way many ripples, many waves, are all the time moving invisibly through the cosmos. These are caused by the actions of beings. And it is to bring order and harmony to all this ocean of activity that karma exists. Karma is nothing else but the wise and loving dispensation of the Creator to bring back the original order and harmony of his creation – if you like, to restore paradise, if I can put it like that, my friend and brother. Just as you can read in the Bible, in Genesis, how God created the heavens and the earth, so you read how there was, to begin with, a state of paradise, a state in which all beings were in perfect harmony. However, this state was lost because not all beings wished to follow divine laws, shall we say. Or, to put it another way, they did not wish to follow the Word of God. There was a revolt in the heavens, and certain beings went their own way, in opposition to the plan of creation which had been envisaged by the Creator. And so the possibility for discord, for deviance from the original blueprint, so to speak, came about. At the same time, the Creator created the laws by which such discord could eventually be overcome. This is what we are talking about as karma.

So, my friend and brother, I have given you much to think about with this teaching. You will begin to appreciate that karma really is a universal law in the truest sense of the word, for it applies to all beings, not just human beings living on earth. But it is, fundamentally, a law which will in time bring about a new harmony, a new paradise, in which all beings on all levels will find a way of living that is completely in harmony with the Creator of the cosmos. On earth, there is the particular challenge that is unique to your planet because you enjoy free will. This free will, in the sense that you know it, does not belong to the other beings in the universe in the same way. But this will be the subject of the next chapter in this book, and therefore we will not discuss it further now. So, with this I leave my love and blessings with you.

All blessings, Philip

Bob: Thank you, Philip. I will, when I've read carefully what you've given here, ask questions and see who will step forward to answer them.

Philip: Yes, that is good, because it is important that a true understanding of all its many facets is achieved. All blessings.

Bob: Philip, just one question still here, please. There will be many who read this chapter and very much question that an angel can come through to bring such teachings. Spirit guides, as discarnate human beings, are one thing, but angels are of a different order. So, what would you say to such readers, Philip?

Philip: Bob, my friend and brother, I will say the following: Why should angels not speak with human beings? After all, there are many instances and examples, are there not, of angels, or even of archangels, giving messages to those who live on earth? If people give due consideration to this, they will find that it is perfectly reasonable to allow such things as possible. Of course, we concede that not all human beings are open to direct angelic contacts. This is true. Not all human beings can receive our words as you can, my friend and brother. Nonetheless, that this can and does take place under certain circumstances is a fact of life. So, we hope that there will indeed be an openness from those who read this book, this chapter, towards this possibility. Because in truth we can have dialogue with our human brothers and sisters when the conditions are right for this. We hope this answers your question.

Love and blessings from Philip.

Bob: Thank you, Philip. Yes, I hope this also for those who read it.

Questions

Bob: Joshua, I would like to put some questions on our theme this morning. Who will step forward to answer them?

Joshua: Red Cloud wishes to do this, my friend.

Bob: Thank you. Then I'll put my questions to him. Red Cloud, Philip tells me that karma truly is universal and effects all beings everywhere. Do you agree with this?

Red Cloud: Bob, my friend, yes, I do agree with what Philip has told you. Everyone, every being, is subject to the law of karma, because it is the means of bringing about true justice and harmony in God's universe. Through this law, all is brought back into cosmic order and cosmic harmony.

Bob: Right. Well then, this seems clear, but I can imagine that in its application to all manner of actions and events, it's really quite complicated – not so?

Red Cloud: Yes, it is in that sense. But on another level, it is relatively straightforward. What do I mean by this? I mean, my friend, that in principle it is straightforward, namely, when seen as the great law of 'cause and effect'. Some cause, whatever it may be, results in an effect or effects. In this sense, it is straightforward, but, as you say, when looked at in its detailed application, then it can appear complicated. So, both of these points are correct.

Bob: Of course, a main question is about the different sorts of karma, if I can put it like this. The most obvious is the differentiation between past and future karma. If one only thinks of past karma affecting a person, then it is a very fatalistic viewpoint. But the moment we think of karma as being ever in creation, creating a new future, it is an entirely different picture, isn't it?

Red Cloud: Indeed, it is, my friend. Yes, just these two views of karma have influenced whole cultures and religious beliefs. Usually it's the past karma, the deterministic scenario, which has been most strongly held by certain dogmas. For example, the Catholic Church's view on hellfire and eternal damnation for sins committed (against the Church!) has influenced countless millions through the ages. Not that the Roman Church used the word 'karma' as such, but still, the cause-and-effect connection was clearly there.

On the other hand, the much more optimistic and uplifting view of karma as creating new future possibilities in a progressive way has so far received short shrift. Nonetheless, this is really the most important aspect of karma going forwards.

Bob: Yes, Red Cloud, I think this fully accords with Christ's impulse for the whole of earth's evolution, does it not? I mean, in the sense that through Christ's intervention, we altogether have a future?

Red Cloud: Yes, my friend, you are right in this. Because the Son of God came to live on the earth and united himself with us all, everything has to be seen in a new light. A new karmic light as well. Remember, he died to absolve the sins of human beings, so that the earth as a whole could continue into the future. Without his intervention, the earth would have been doomed, we must say, because the weight of sin would have dragged it into the abyss.

Bob: As I understand it through Rudolf Steiner's work, this has to do with the combined effects of negative human actions on the planet, on Mother Earth. This is what Christ dealt with, so to speak. But individually, we still have to deal with, and take responsibility for, our own actions – *all* our actions. Correct?

Red Cloud: This is absolutely correct, my friend. Yes, each person has to reap whatever they sow, and then see how they deal with that fruit.

Bob: When we look at karma in its widest sense, beyond just the human realm, then there are of course very many questions that could be asked. For example, how karma applies to the animal kingdom, or even the plants and minerals. Also, how it applies to the higher spiritual beings. There are a lot of possible questions, aren't there?

Red Cloud: There are indeed. There is no shortage of avenues of enquiry. However, in one chapter you can only cover so much.

Bob: Well, let me just ask how that is with our nature kingdoms, since these are very much threatened through our own human actions and global warming, climate changes, etc.

Red Cloud: Yes, in this you are correct. Very grave dangers do threaten all the realms of nature, because of what human beings have set in motion. From the point of view of karma, this is all very complicated, one would have to say. Yes, in some ways it does seem straightforward. Let us say that a particular animal species is threatened with destruction because of human actions. Yes, that is the end of that particular animal type. But the consequences of that are yet to be truly felt and accounted for. So, it is one thing to see what happens on a purely earthly level of occurrence, and it is another thing to appreciate what this means on other planes or levels of being.

This is where it becomes most involved, because the karmic consequences are multidimensional. And this will also apply to the plant kingdom, and even to the mineral realm. Things are interconnected, and the results of actions done (or not done) are multitudinous. It is not just a simple, linear 'A causes B' approach when you are looking at these realities. And remember, my friend, that behind all manifestations are actually beings. The world, the cosmos, is one of beings, not things. So, karma and its effects affect beings on all different levels.

Bob: Well, it seems clear, Red Cloud, that to do karma justice would actually require a whole book. Yes, this is such a book, but what I mean is that to look into details would require a lot more space than we can devote to it here, right?

Red Cloud: Yes, that is quite right. It is one thing to consider how it applies to human beings, which is what this book is mainly about, and it is another thing to extend its scope over the entire cosmos!

Bob: So, unless you still have something important to add, Red Cloud, I think I'll bring this chapter to a close.

Red Cloud: Yes. The only thing I would still add, or point out rather, is that through a right understanding of karma, human beings will gain a much deeper and wider appreciation of their actions for the universe as a whole. After all, the planet on which you live is meant to become a shining star of love, radiating into space, into the depths of the cosmos. To achieve that aim, people will need to become much more awake to the true consequences of their actions. So, this is the great challenge which karma sets before us all.

All blessings, Red Cloud

Bob: Thank you.

8
KARMA IN FREEDOM

Bob: Joshua, can I see if one of the guides will step forward for the teaching on this theme, please?

Joshua: Shalom, my friend. Yes, of course, a guide is there to help. Markos is here for you.

Bob: Thank you. Markos, can you now bring through your teachings, please?

Teachings

Markos: My friend, it is once again a great pleasure to work with you, and I will speak on this theme of 'karma in freedom' today. Now, let me say to start with that there are many misconceptions to do with karma, and also many misconceptions to do with freedom. So, when we combine both terms, we risk a double jeopardy, so to speak! That is to say, that we risk getting into very deep water, unless we have complete clarity about what we're speaking about. You see, my friend, 'karma' is not contradictory to 'freedom', as many imagine, and neither is freedom at loggerheads with karma. No, this only appears to be so when neither are adequately understood. Therefore, in this teaching today, let us be as clear as we can about what we are really addressing.

So, a major misunderstanding about karma is that it is predestined and unbending, in the sense that it is fixed down. According to this conception, which is incorrect, a person's karma is 'set in stone' and cannot be changed or altered in any way – your karma is your destiny, your fate, and that's that. There is nothing to be done but to accept it and submit to it.

But karma is not like that in reality. Karma is flexible and is open to many possibilities in order to fulfil its aims and goals. Therefore, to think that it is rigid only reflects a fixed idea. Karma is constantly creative; it is able continually to create new paths, new avenues, through which what needs to come about can be enacted. So, this was the first thing to set straight.

Secondly, if we turn to 'freedom' *per se*, this is not what many people think it is. It is not about just doing what you want to do at any moment in time, because these wants are often, mostly, prompted by desires and wishes that spring from unknown sources deep within the person's soul constitution. This is not true freedom, because true freedom has to spring from wide-awake consciousness, and not from out of dark, unconscious depths. Freedom lives in the light, not in the darkness. So, to experience such freedom, a person needs to be free of impulses, desires, wants and wishes which really spring from our emotional or instinctive natures. Moreover, it is not simply an 'outer' freedom of action that is the hallmark of true freedom, but a deep, inner freedom of the spirit. It is a state of mind in which the individual is not influenced by all manner of wishes, desires and wants.

Freedom is really an inner, spiritual activity in which the person's true self is able to find expression. This can also be expressed in truly altruistic and selfless outer action. Not an action which gives a reward to the actor, but which is given as a service to others. To truly serve a need in the world is an act of true freedom. So now, my friend, when we combine both of these elements, karma and freedom, in the true way, without all the misconceptions, then we see that they are entirely compatible with each other. We create new karma, original karma, out of our true freedom. And when we remember that the law of karma is really the 'law of love' in action, then we see that freedom and love are the highest ideals to which a person can aspire.

In other words, we are truly free when we love the action which we perform out of love itself. In doing this, we create a stream of karma which leads us into the future in the best possible way. Now, my friend, what I have given here as teaching is something to be pondered and to be understood on deeper levels of being. But on the other hand, whenever anyone actually commits selfless deeds, deeds that are not done to benefit the one who acts, then we already see new karma being created. The act of creation is already before us in such instances.

This, then, is the fundamental and essential nature of 'karma in freedom'. It is that which gives each of us the opportunity to create the future that we dream of, provided it is a dream which serves the highest good of all beings.

Of course, it is also true to say that not so many people can put this into practice, at least not all the time. This is part of the great school of life that every person is engaged in, whether they realize it or not. So, it is truly a work-in-progress for those who wish to be of service to others. All who strive to do what is good and right – though 'right' should not be seen in any narrow, dogmatic sense – are actively engaged in the process of creating karma in freedom. The more people who can aspire to this and actually do it, the better it is for the world as a whole.

So my friend, I hope that what I have said today is understandable to you and those who will read these words.

All blessings, Markos

Bob: Thank you, Markos. I will read carefully what you have given, and then see what questions I can ask.
Markos: Good, we shall look forward to these. All blessings.

Questions

Bob: Joshua, can we see this morning who would like to answer my questions?
Joshua: Yes, we can – and already Pierre is stepping forward for this task.
Bob: Right, thank you. Pierre, I think the theme of 'karma in freedom' does beg many questions, so I'll try to bring them forward. Firstly, 'freedom' can perhaps mean different things to different people. We can speak about outer physical freedom, to move from place to place. We could speak about emotional freedom or mental freedom, where constraints and limitations are lifted. Yes, we can also speak of spiritual freedom, which perhaps might be reflected in 'free speech'. So, different levels and layers of freedom, not so?

Pierre: Yes indeed, my friend. All that is correct. Freedom is a central concern, a central issue, in many spheres of life. It is the opposite of being imprisoned into a place or space where movement is impossible. So, freedom has to do with movement: I would say, the ability to move in one way or another, instead of being fixed down.

Bob: Yes, and this then relates to karma, doesn't it? Because karma is also a movement, a dynamic process.

Pierre: Yes, it is precisely that. Karma is always seeking ways to bring about balance in a person's life situation. And balance in that sense is also a healing process. So, you could say that karma brings healing, true healing to a situation – to a situation of destiny.

Bob: Pierre, I think when we talk about such things there is a danger of becoming too philosophical and abstract for many people. Is it possible to keep things simple?

Pierre: Well, my friend, yes, to some extent it is. The problem is, of course, that life is usually rather complicated! So, although we can always try to simplify matters, the reality is very often not so simple.

Bob: True. Is the relationship between karma and freedom a different concern, a different issue, at different ages and stages of a person's life, say for a child and an adult, for example? Or for people from different cultural backgrounds?

Pierre: Certainly, this is the case. Obviously, for a child, the question of freedom is a very practical one and usually related to his or her desires and wants of the moment. The child wants a particular toy and is not able to have it just then, so he or she feels very upset, very unfree to fulfil that desire. Perhaps this is not so different, however, also for adults? After all, the object of the desires may be different from when the person was a child, but the internal compulsion remains much the same.

With regard to different cultures and backgrounds, here again it all depends on what has been considered to be normal and typical for that culture, because we are all 'conditioned', shaped and formed, by the culture we grow up in. Africa will be very different from Europe, which again will be different from North America, and so on. So lots of variations exist.

However, that being said, the concept and wish for 'freedom' is very widespread and universal in humanity.

Bob: Yes, I can see that. So maybe the main question, Pierre, is again: 'Is freedom compatible with the working of karma in human life?'

Pierre: Yes, it is fully compatible. Karma, as we have learnt in this book, is the God-given means of bringing about harmony, balance and order into the cosmos. It constantly brings about the needed balancing act, so that actions performed at one moment of time can have the consequences expressed at other times, in a way that enables the balance to be restored. And in this balance, we also find the conditions which enable true freedom to exist. To be free, you must also be in balance, because otherwise you are constrained, restricted, by an imbalanced situation. So you could say that freedom exists in a perfect state of balance. And this perfect state of balance is really a state of pure love. Love restores all things into balance. Thereby you are also left entirely spiritually free.

So in a nutshell, karma and freedom both aim for the same goal. Namely, to enable love to come about as the most important goal of our existence, whether on earth or in heaven, so to speak. Love is the key which unites freedom and karma and evolution.

Bob: Well, Pierre, I think with all this I have a lot to think about and digest!

Pierre: Yes, my friend, you probably do.

All blessings, Pierre

9
KARMA IN CLIMATE CHANGE

Bob: Joshua, today I would like to turn to the very important theme of this chapter. As I write these words, the final stages of the COP26 conference on climate change are taking place in Scotland. It is likely that, after two weeks of discussions, the final outcome of this meeting will still fall well below the expectations and hopes of most people worldwide. Can you tell me, Joshua, which guide wishes to bring through teachings on this theme today?

Joshua: Shalom, my friend. Yes, it is indeed Pan himself, the God of nature, who would wish to address this theme.

Bob: Thank you. When I am ready, I will sit to receive what Pan can give me.

*

Bob: Well, since I spoke with Joshua this morning, it is now evening. Can I ask you, Pan, if you do in fact wish to come through with teachings?

Pan: My friend, indeed I do. Yes, I am Pan, the 'God of Nature' so-called, and I am happy to bring through the teaching for this chapter.

Bob: Thank you. Please go ahead.

Teachings

Pan: Well, my friend, I said I am happy to bring through the teachings, but actually I do so with a heavy heart. Why is this? It is because the natural world is in crisis, and it is a crisis that has been brought about by the actions of mankind. Yes, humanity, the human race, has brought nature to her knees, so to speak. I mean by this that what was once the natural and harmonious order of things has been completely disrupted by the thoughtless and selfish nature of man. This is a matter of great concern for myself and for all those nature spirits and elementals who work tirelessly in nature. We are extremely pessimistic about the willingness of human beings to bring about the changes that will be required – are required now – in order to try to restore balance and harmony.

We look with hope, that is ever diminishing in strength, to see these changes enacted. Instead of this, we see all the leaders, at least all those in the positions of greatest power in the world, dragging their feet. Yes, dragging their feet, even as they see disaster after disaster unfolding before their very eyes. How blind can they be?

Yes, we know that many words are spoken in great conferences and meetings, but these words have little or no substance in them when it comes to decisive actions. This state of affairs is causing us much pain and anguish. It is not our doing that the oceans rise up, or that the fires burn relentlessly, or that drought and famine follow on, or that the rains fall interminably. No, we do not implement or initiate such things – *you* do!

Even with the best will in the world, we cannot prevent these catastrophes from taking place. It doesn't lie in our power to change things for the better without the active cooperation of human beings.

Yes, it is cooperation which is needed on all fronts and in every way that is possible. If this were forthcoming, then indeed we can help to remedy things and to do our best to restore equilibrium and balance back into the kingdoms of nature. But believe me, time is running out very fast to make the necessary adjustments. Once the ice sheets have melted, there is no way of putting them back in place. Once the forests have been hacked down and destroyed, there is no way to grow hundred-year-old trees in a decade or two. Once the soil has been stripped of its nutrients and minerals, there is no way in which it can be readily replenished. And so the list goes on and on.

Do people know about these things? Yes, they do. Do they care about these things? No, in most cases they don't. Yes, we concede that those most closely and immediately affected do care. After all, very often their very lives are threatened, or hang in the balance. Yes, these ordinary people *do* care, but those who sit in power prevaricate and, rather, try to see how to preserve their status and power positions than to make the sacrifices required. Yet these are not really sacrifices, because looked at in the longer term, the rewards for all, for everyone, far outweigh the short-term cutbacks and limitations.

So, my friend, you will realize from all that I have said so far that we are very, very worried where the world is heading, and at top speed! It will be of no use looking back in a decade's time and saying, 'Oh, I wish we had

67

done more'. By then, the damage is done. The ice has melted, the temperatures are rising, and the extreme weather and climate conditions will be even more widespread and devastating than they are already.

This, my friends, is the karma, the consequences, which you yourselves are putting into place. Yes, karma, world karma, which affects all life forms on the earth, comes about through the deeds you do or don't do today. Karma is continually created. Whether it is good or bad, constructive or destructive, wholesome or sickening, depends entirely on you as a human race. We as spirit beings, who sustain nature in all its infinitude of forms, are dependent on you. We know what to do to cause the plants to grow and thrive. We know what to do to bring health and strength to the various species of animals. We know how to form and consolidate the minerals and crystal forms in the solid earth. Yes, we have a great knowledge of all these natural, life-sustaining processes, but without your cooperation, our hands are being tied.

Yes, this should impress upon you all the power which you wield and, at the same time, the tremendous responsibility which you carry for the health and well-being of the whole planet.

Oh yes, you say: 'We know that the planet has gone through ups and downs before, and look, it has pulled through, it is still here.' Yes indeed, in that you are correct. There have been great upheavals and cataclysms in the past, it is quite true. But, my friends, the one which is facing you now is truly of your own making, and therefore the responsibility which you bear towards it exceeds all former catastrophes upon Mother Earth.

Other factors and forces brought about these cataclysms. They are not the same ones which prevail today in the twenty-first century. Now you are bringing about a great man-made catastrophe with your eyes wide open. You know what you are doing! Does not that beggar belief? How is it possible, we ask ourselves, that human beings can be so foolish as to willingly destroy the very fabric of life on which they depend? How can it be that you willingly destroy yourselves? And to think: 'Oh, we have plenty of time left to make the changes, in a year or two, or a decade or two, or even more.' Well, in this you again demonstrate your foolishness.

Well, my friends, let us consider what you can do *now* to help us restore order in nature. You can cut the emissions of all those gases which are creating a blanket around the earth planet, and gradually, or rather quickly, stifling her. You can stop cutting down all the trees, and instead protect what you still have left of the great forests, the lungs of the world. You can stop polluting the seas and oceans and the soil with all the rubbish which you thoughtlessly dispose of. You can stop treating nature in all her forms as if she is some commodity, some*thing* to be exploited and usurped of all her riches and wealth. You can instead become true custodians and guardians of Mother Earth, as 'the gods' you are meant to become.

Yes, my friends, I do not use that word 'gods' lightly. But I cannot but help use it, because that is written into the great plan of Creation by the all-world Creator Being of this universe, this cosmos. This is what you have been destined to become ever since the earth planet came into being, millions of your earth years ago.

69

But when will you awaken to your true cosmic heritage? When will you realize that the future lies in your own hands? Yes, the karma of the past has led you to the heights of consciousness, self-consciousness, which you have reached. It was your karma, your destiny to become self-actualized sentient beings, in a way which no other beings on the earth were destined to become. This was your heritage and the gift bestowed upon you by our father, the Creator. But this heritage, which includes your power of self-determination and free will, must be realized, united with a great sense of responsibility for what is to come. For what *you* are creating as your future. Yes, your future, which even now is being mapped out by your actions and deeds.

And so, my friends, we would implore you to grasp the nettle, so to speak, in order to do that which is needed for the future of the planet, which is your earthly home. Yes, it is true that your real home is in the spirit worlds. This is true, but your evolution as a race, your progress to become gods, has to be enacted through your lives on planet earth. There is no other way for you to achieve your goal, even though that goal is known only to the most advanced among you: the goal, that the earth truly becomes a shining star of love that will radiate into the cosmos and bring hope to all beings, both earthly and heavenly. This is the great goal and aim of your evolutionary journey, but to succeed in this, you need Mother Earth as your place of abode, as the place where the great transformation is to be enacted. With this image in front of you, I will draw my teachings to a close.

All blessings, Pan

70

Bob: Thank you, Pan. I hope I have brought through aright the words you have spoken?

Pan: Have no fear, my friend. You have indeed been a good scribe for the teachings I wished to bring – wished to bring with all my heart, because there is no time to lose.

Questions

Bob: Dear Pan, as I write these words, the delegates at the United Nations COP26 conference are trying to reach a final written agreement which all the countries represented can agree to. That is to say, nearly 200 countries, big and small, from the so-called 'developed' and 'developing' world are endeavouring to reach a consensus. Even though the third draft of this agreement is far from perfect in its various parts, still it is hoped that a spirit of compromise, for the sake of the whole world community and for the health of the planet, will be signed off today, 13 November 2021. So, what do *you* think about all this, Pan?

Pan: My friend, I think it does not go anywhere near far enough to address the crisis facing the human race, and indeed all life forms on the planet. There is too much in the way of politics and national vested interests in these deliberations. It would need a far more selfless and altruistic attitude from all parties involved if disasters are to be minimized.

Disasters will take place due to global warming and the resultant climate changes. This is for certain. The only thing that can and should be done is to find ways to minimize their impacts around the globe.

So, in short, I would say this is too little too late!

Bob: Pan, I do accept that what you say is right, but surely leaders, politicians and ordinary people cannot make decisive changes overnight? To reduce carbon emissions into the atmosphere, to reduce or stop the use of fossil fuels, to develop and distribute 'green' energy production – all these things take time, don't they?

Pan: Yes, they do indeed, but the real question is how much time do you have left to make the changes which are needed? And I can tell you, my friend, the time is fast running out. The detrimental effects of global warming are going to hit you much quicker than the current predictions. Things will speed up, will accelerate, at a rate that will take even your clever climate scientists by surprise. We in spirit can already see all these things playing out. We can see the disasters which are just waiting to happen, to manifest on the earthly plane. And this is why we say, too little too late. It is not that we do not applaud the efforts being made by those who are most sincere and most motivated, but this itself is not enough.

Bob: Pan, can't you and other spirit beings push us along quicker? Can't you somehow intervene, knowing what you do from your vantage point, to get us to action now?

Pan: No, unfortunately we can't do this. Human beings have free will, and we must respect this, according to Divine Law. Therefore, we cannot intervene, in the sense of coercing anyone to do anything. We can only help, support and assist when you yourselves have made your own decisions.

Bob: So, what bearing does all this have on the theme of karma?

Pan: Well, karma is a universal law which affects all beings in the cosmos, both human and spirit beings. No one is exempt from it. However, human beings are in a position to create karma. Karma is not fatalistic, and it is not already set in stone in the sense that it is unchanging and rigid. No, it is mobile, creative and subject to the actions that are performed. So, in the case of global warming, if certain actions are not done, then inevitably there will be consequences set in motion for future times. However, if the right actions are performed when they are really needed, then that future will be formed differently.

Bob: Okay, Pan, but you said that already you and other beings can see the impending disasters. So, how is that? Are they inevitable?

Pan: Yes and no. Yes, if the present course of inaction is followed, and no, if the right interventions are made *now*.

Bob: But given that karma, world karma, is mobile and creative, can't we change the 'doom and gloom' scenario a bit later, say in a decade or two, or three, rather than have everything working perfectly right now?

Pan: Well, my friend, the window, the opportunity for effective changes to be made is limited. It is not as long as a piece of string! Rather, there is a period of time in which it is still possible to do what is needed, but beyond that, there is no turning back the clock.

Bob: Tell me, Pan, when a group of human beings gather, as at COP26, to try to work together and cooperate, are there also invisible, spirit beings gathered there? Maybe even you yourself, Pan?

Pan: Oh yes, this is of course true. Many beings are present at such an occasion, and yes, this does include me. How could I stay away from such an important event?

Bob: And might some people on earth, who are more spiritually sensitive, maybe even clairvoyant, be aware that others are there?

Pan: Again, yes, this is true. There will be those people, probably few and far between, who are well aware that invisible friends are present and looking on.

Bob: Can such people, or others also perhaps, be influenced by spirit? I mean, to help get the most helpful imaginations, inspirations and intuitions. Is this possible?

Pan: Yes, of course this is possible, provided that whatever help we give is in response to a request, a freewill request.

Bob: Well, I can imagine that there will be some people present who are praying for just such help, not so?

Pan: Yes, some. But not as many as you might imagine, I'm afraid. It does need a certain degree of spiritual development to be able to receive such contents.

Bob: Yes, I guess that is so. Well, Pan, there are probably many more questions that could be asked, but can I ask you, what would you say is most important now?

Pan: Action, action, action. Nothing is more important than to get on with what needs doing. After the talking, after the formulations of a common agreement, then urgent and decisive actions are needed. Nothing less than this will be able to avert the worst which is yet to come.

Bob: So, this really is a pretty stark warning, isn't it?

Pan: Yes, my friend, and this is why I am happy to have been allowed to speak on all this in your new book.

Bob: Well, your presence and input, Pan, seems to me essential. Do you speak on behalf of all the nature spirits and the elementals of earth, air, fire and water?

Pan: Indeed, I do. All my subjects are yearning for human beings to wake up to their responsibilities. All wish to see a decisive change, for the good of the whole world.

Bob: And will you, Pan, and your many subjects, work with us in cooperation if we recognize and turn to you?

Pan: We will, we will, we will. Even if you do not recognize us *per se*, if people do the right things, then we are working with you all the way.

Bob: Pan, on this very positive note I will bring this session to a close. Thank you.

Pan: Thank you, my friend.

*

Bob: Dear Pan, I would like to ask you further for your comments on the following. Namely, that your tone and content regarding climate change in this current book is more directly looking at the material, physical effects of our human activities, in contrast to your contribution in my earlier book.* Previously, you pointed more to the importance of *spiritual* awareness and awakening, rather than focusing on the very physical aspects. Why is there this seeming polarity in your contributions on this subject?

Pan: Bob, my friend, they are two sides of the same coin. They belong fundamentally together. Yes, it is absolutely true that a new spiritual awareness needs to come about, but it is equally true that decisions concerning the very practical, material steps to help reverse the effects of

---

*See *Knowledge of Spirit Worlds and Life After Death*, Clairview Books 2020, pp. 99-102.

climate change also need to be made. So, really both these aspects belong together. What use will be an enhanced spiritual awareness if this is not then translated into physical actions for the good of the whole world? On the other hand, just to do the physical changes without an evolving spiritual consciousness will also be rather short-lived and inadequate. Yes, both a new perception and new actions need to take place in order to effect decisive changes for the future of the planet and all its life forms. I hope with this I have helped to clarify this matter for you.

All blessings, Pan

Bob: Joshua, can you confirm for me that I was indeed receiving communications from Pan just now?
Joshua: Shalom, my friend. Yes, I can confirm this. Pan was most anxious to answer your question to the best of his ability.

All blessings, Joshua

Postscript

The COP26 conference took place in Glasgow, Scotland. To the east of Glasgow is Edinburgh, and this was the place where Robert Ogilvy Crombie was born, and where, in 1966, in a park, he had his first direct meeting with the nature spirits. In the book *Encounters with Nature Spirits, Co-creating with the Elemental Kingdom*, we read of his meetings with Pan. Amongst the conversations which Crombie had with Pan, we find the following words:

Communicating with my subjects is not a garden game for the odd half hour, when there is nothing better to do. It is of vital importance for the survival of mankind. Unless humanity comes to realize the dangerous stupidity of outraging nature and stops the ever-increasing rate of pollution, it will ultimately destroy itself.*

These sobering words of Pan, from the early 1970s, ring even truer to us in 2021, half a century later, when we stand at the very brink of disaster.

---

*Robert Ogilvy Crombie, *Encounters with Nature Spirits: Co-creating with the Elemental Kingdom*, Findhorn Press 2018, p. 83.

10
KARMA IN CONFLICT

Bob: Dear Joshua, in view of all that is taking place in the world in May 2022, I feel that I should include this additional chapter in the book. Do you agree?

Joshua: Shalom, my friend. Yes, we do agree, since there is a need to see things that are happening within a wider perspective.

Bob: Well, I will see who wishes to give us some teachings on this theme.

Joshua: Yes, Raja Lampa wishes to do this for you.

Bob: Thank you, Raja.

Teachings

Raja Lampa: Yes, my friend, we well understand why you feel a certain definite impulse to include this theme in your new book. There are certainly dire circumstances being acted out on planet earth today, with various conflicts raging in different parts of the world.

Of course, we realize that it is very much the war in Ukraine that is the centre of your attention at present, but also bear in mind that this is not the only conflict that is taking place.

So, let us consider what the theme of 'karma in conflict' actually means. It means that when any conflict comes about, be it between individual people or between nations, that karma is being played out. We mean this in a serious way, even though the phrase 'played out' was used. Because, my friend, there is a complicated and involved set of factors at play in such circumstances. This is true whether the conflict ensues on a small scale or on a large scale. Factors from the past and factors leading into a new future are intermingling in such conflict situations.

If we turn to the larger-scale conflicts that can happen, that is to say, essentially a war type of situation, where one side battles against the other, then we have to be mindful of all that is involved on various different levels. There is of course the political, earthly level of the conflict, of the war. That is there on the one hand, but there are also other important or significant levels that are playing out at the same time. These include the soul and spiritual levels, as well as the purely physical level which everyone can see with their ordinary eyes. Yes, there are different levels, different dimensions, to such terrible conflicts of interest, of power, of aspirations and intentions. On the level of intentions, you straightaway come into the soul, and even the spiritual levels. Yes, you can, of course, also speak about the differing ideologies and cultural and spiritual points-of-view. And so you see that the conflict is happening on all these different levels at the same time. The purely physical level is only one of these. True, it is the level that captures everyone's attention, since people, soldiers, are being killed and wounded on both sides. However, there are also deeper levels to such struggles that are taking place on quite other dimensions.

So in terms of karma, you can begin to imagine that various strands are being woven through the conflict situations. Strands that are not at all limited to the physical plane only, but take effect on the levels of soul and spirit too. These karmic consequences, as we may call them, can be, and often are, very far-reaching and can last for generations to come. In other words, destinies are being forged out of the fire of the conflicts. Destinies which affect, and will continue to affect, whole peoples for generations to come. What people will do about these things, how they will handle them, how they will learn from them, will very much determine how the relationships between the peoples involved, perhaps on a national level, will play out in future.

Karma always gives the opportunities for growth, for development, for recompense, for forgiveness, for evolution to unfold. Karma is there to create a new harmony, a new set of circumstances, which can help heal old wounds and rifts. Karma leads us into the future to create a better world for all, and this should be the outcome – the best outcome – for all conflict situations, be they on the individual level or on the national or international level.

Human beings often have to learn their hardest lessons through the hardest of conditions, and conflicts or wars provide a case in point. Terrible things can and do happen in wars, but these can eventually lead to a greater good if lessons are learned on all sides. Yes, karma in that sense is a force for good – a force that helps to bring about a new harmony and the possibilities for peaceful coexistence and true cooperation between people on planet earth.

So, with this I will bring my teachings to a close, and we will await the questions which you will no doubt wish to ask us.

All blessings, Raja Lampa

Bob: Thank you. Yes, when I have had time to read carefully what has been given here, I will then see which questions to raise.

Questions

Bob: Joshua, I am ready to put some questions to the guides on this theme. Is this all right?

Joshua: Shalom, my friend. Yes, it is perfectly all right with us. Let us see who wishes to step forward.

Pierre: Yes, please let me step in here to answer your questions.

Bob: Right, Pierre. Now, I understand from what Raja Lampa said that we need to understand conflicts happening on various different levels and not just on the physical one?

Pierre: Yes, my friend, that is correct. Just as when you confront someone, it is not just your physical body state that is involved, but also your emotions and your thoughts come into play as well.

Bob: Yes, that is of course clear, and in that sense the battle, so to speak, takes place in all these several ways at the same time?

Pierre: Yes, that is correct, and that is why it is so important to look beyond the merely physical side of things, however dramatic and unnerving that may be.

Bob: Well, if I think now of the pictures and images coming in the television reports of the war in Ukraine, then certainly the physical devastation and horrors of the war are very striking indeed. However, as you say, Pierre, there is also a tremendous clash of emotions and feelings and of thoughts that accompany all this.

Pierre: Yes, they do, and of course you need to consider what has really sparked this war into operation; what the causes are that have led to the physical conflict itself?

Bob: Well, there may be various views about this – the causes, that is – but certainly I would think that fear has a large part in this.

Pierre: Yes, it certainly does, my friend. Whenever someone feels threatened, feels fearful, then this can be the real cause for aggression to take place. But behind the aggression, behind the physical onslaught, there is a deep fear that underpins such actions.

Bob: But Pierre, if we try to see what is happening in the light of karma, which is after all the theme of this chapter, how can we better understand such a conflict?

Pierre: Well, in the light of karma, in the light that events are being acted out which have long-term consequences for everyone who is involved, we can begin to see that whatever the physical outcome of those courses of action, there will be consequences also on deeper levels. Now, what do I mean by this? I mean that in order for karma to find ways to bring about balance, healing and redemption, it will require all parties involved in the current conflict to get together and find a new way forward. After all, such a war cannot go on forever. It has a beginning, and it must also have an end. However, the end will only come when one side is stronger and the other side capitulates, or when there is a stalemate with neither side able to take the upper hand. At any event, whichever scenario comes about, it is always a matter of people sitting around a table and working out a solution to their problems. This is true both of small-scale and large-scale conflict situations. At some point, negotiations are required and compromises have to be made in order to find a way forward: a way to bring about a peaceful coexistence, in spite of all that has gone on before. There really is no other way.

Bob: Yes, Pierre, I can accept what you say here, but this may be a very bitter pill to swallow – not so?

Pierre: Yes indeed, my friend, it usually is. But really, there is no other choice, because otherwise the wound continues to fester and will eventually bring about yet another conflict in the future.

Bob: Pierre, in terms of karma, I suppose the present conflict between Russia and Ukraine, can be seen as rooted in their past relationships, not so?

Pierre: Yes of course, that is the case. Only by appreciating how the relationship between these two nations has evolved over time can we really grasp what is taking place now. However, how that will be in the future depends entirely on how they can solve their current problems. This lies in the hands of those who are the appointed leaders of their peoples. And depending upon the decisions which these leaders make, so the fate of their nations will unfold. Of course, one would hope for wisdom to prevail, though we know that too often power and politics are ruling the day. However, the karmic consequences of what is decided upon cannot be avoided. We are of course here dealing with the destiny of whole nations rather than simply with individuals.

Bob: I'm not sure what else I can ask, but one thing does occur to me… Can we really speak in such a situation of good versus evil? I mean, can it be seen that there really is a clash between forces of good and evil taking place?

Pierre: It is certainly possible to see events in that context. However, what one side might see as evil, the other side might see as good.

Bob: Yes Pierre, but surely that is just semantics. The reality on the ground will make it clear whether good or evil is being perpetrated, not so?

Pierre: Yes, that is of course the case. However, whether something is inspired by good or evil forces also depends on where one stands. I mean to say that this has to be seen from both sides, not merely from the one perspective.

Bob: Well Pierre, this could sound rather too platonic, too abstract, when you actually see or hear of the atrocities committed in this war?

Pierre: Yes, it could indeed, but there are always at least two sides to any dispute, and it is necessary to view these dispassionately in order to see, on a deeper level, what is really going on.

Bob: Joshua, at this point I have to ask you if I am still properly in touch with Pierre? Am I still receiving the communications correctly?

Joshua: Shalom, my friend. Yes you are, but we do realize that in discussing such an emotive subject as this, it can sound too abstract for you. Nonetheless, it is necessary to step back in order to view events on the ground from a higher perspective.

Bob: Yes, this may well be so, Joshua, but what happens on the ground level is pretty gruesome to hear about!

Joshua: Yes, it is. Nonetheless, wars are taking place on different levels and, karmically speaking, will lead to consequences that will always try to find a balance and create a new healing within the whole.

Bob: Well in that case, Joshua, I suppose we really need to see how events actually unfold, in order to be able to make a better, more complete judgement in the future?

Joshua: Yes, that is so. Only when the dust has settled, only when a new peace comes about, will it be possible to assess all that has happened in a new light.

Bob: Very well, Joshua and Pierre, I will now bring this chapter to a close. Thank you.

Joshua: Thank you, my friend. All blessings.

Bob: Actually, Joshua, I should still ask a further question… This has to do with the fact that the present conflict in Ukraine is not simply being fought on a national level, but also it is having big international consequences. So, isn't this affecting world karma, almost comparable to the two world wars of the twentieth century?

Joshua: Shalom, my friend. Yes, you are correct in this. The world has become a smaller place, so to speak, because of the modern means of communication and the interconnections on the financial and economic levels. Therefore, such a conflict happening in a particular geographical locality spreads out its effects on a worldwide basis. This in itself highlights how everything is connected and interconnected. Karmically, this also means that the implications of these events will be felt throughout the whole world and will change things in ways that could not be imagined beforehand.

Bob: So, could this actually all be turned to the good? I mean, in spite of the terrible things now happening, could something, a greater good, emerge from all this suffering and pain and desolation?

Joshua: Yes, indeed it could, because a very hard lesson is being enacted, a lesson which is man-made, so to speak, but which can lead potentially into an era of greater peace and posterity for all. This is the great enigma, the great conundrum, of such shattering events: that in spite of all the terrible, truly terrible, events taking place, a greater good can emerge for all humanity.

Bob: Well, we can only pray that this will be the case!

Joshua: Yes, indeed, we all pray that this will be the outcome, the karmic outcome of this present world crisis.

All blessings, Joshua

Bob: Thank you.

AFTERWORD

In the Introduction, when I put my initial question to Joshua, asking if the guides would be willing to cooperate with me on this new project, I received a very positive reply. It was left open to see exactly which of them would contribute to the book. Now, looking back, we see that in total, nine guides were involved, that is, if we count both Pan and Philip in that number. In terms of their frequency of making contributions, some of the guides were more active than others, we can say. So, for example, Red Cloud, Markos and Pierre featured much more than Gopi Ananda, Isobel, Pan or Philip. However, this is much less relevant than the fact that everyone willingly contributed to the book as a new research project. For this, I am very grateful.

The format for each chapter – as was suggested by the guides – of receiving teachings on each main theme, followed by the Q and A sessions, worked well, I think. Certainly, all the themes, posed as research questions, are important in helping us to better understand the workings of karma in human life. However, the chapters concerned with the pandemic and with climate change are especially telling. That Pan himself felt called upon to address the latter theme should further underline its urgency for humanity, wherever we happen to be living on the planet. His clear warning that events will overtake us faster than even the experts realize is to be taken very seriously. Cooperation in action from all parties is what is called for now, with the added reassurance that Pan and the whole elemental world of beings will then help us in our endeavours.

Although the notion of karma, and reincarnation for that matter, is sometimes used quite liberally ever since the so-called New Age breakthroughs in the 1960s and 1970s, they really need to be understood as concretely as possible. What the guides have given us here point in the right direction, I believe. If we begin to view the events which happen in our actual lives through this karmic lens, then our sense for a deeper meaning and purpose in these perhaps difficult situations can surely be increased.

Instead of our usual despair, especially over life-changing accidents or illnesses, for example, we may realize that they can also be seen as unique opportunities for personal growth and development. In actual fact, this very positive aspect does often come clearly to the fore when some people have to face a diagnosis of terminal illness. They can then find previously unknown reserves of strength, fortitude and courage, which inspire their friends and family alike. Without the illness, these qualities would probably have lain dormant.

So, I think the most important thing we can take away from the guides' teachings, and live with on a daily basis, is that the karmic 'law of love' is helping us according to our real needs, even if these are hidden from our ordinary consciousness. There is a wise and loving spirit guiding us along our life journeys – journeys which we ourselves, out of our higher spirit beings, have actually planned and orchestrated before we descended into incarnation this time around. Nonetheless, as we have learnt, karma is not to be seen rigidly. It can be satisfied through many possible avenues. As human beings, we do enjoy free will, and therefore also have choices to make, especially at critical moments of our lives. Whatever we decide upon, karma, as a good friend, will work with us to continue to guide us towards our own goals. At the same time, it will ensure that our experiences will bring us towards a new state of balance, harmony and healing.

Ultimately, it will help us to learn gradually to transcend our too-earthly, materialistic selves, as we recognize that, in essence, we are of a spiritual, divine nature. As the guides point out, we are destined to live on a planet which should become a 'star of love', radiating out into the widths of the cosmos. Whether it will actually achieve that sublime goal probably depends very much on all the good karma which we can, working together, create for our future.

So, with that image strongly in mind, I will bring this book to a conclusion and once more thank all the guides for their willingness to bring it about. Thank you.

All blessings,

Bob

APPENDIX

The guides contributing to this book are:

1. *Joshua Isaiah*. In a former life he was a Rabbi.
2. *Red Cloud*. In a former life, he was a chief of the Sioux Native American tribe.
3. *Raja Lampa*. In a former life he was a Tibetan Lama.
4. *Markos*. In a former life he was a Greek monk and philosopher.
5. *Pierre*. In a former life in France, he was a member of the Knights Templar.
6. *Isobel*. She was my pupil in a former lifetime in India, when I was then a guru.
7. *Gopi Ananda*. Likewise, she was also associated with me in a former lifetime in India.
8. *Philip*. My guardian angel.
9. *Pan*. The God of Nature.

FURTHER READING

Alexander, E. (2012) *Proof of Heaven – A Neurosurgeon's Journey into the Afterlife.* Macmillan

Archiati, P. (1997) *Reincarnation in Modern Life.* Temple Lodge Publishing

Butfield, C. and Hughes, T. (2021) *EARTHSHOT – How to Save Our Planet.* John Murray

Cerminara, G. (1971) *Many Mansions.* Neville Spearman

Guirdham, A. (1982) *The Cathars and Reincarnation.* Turnstone Press

Helliwell, T. (1997) *Summer with the Leprechauns.* Blue Dolphin Publishing

Maathai, W. (2010) *Replenishing the Earth.* Doubleday

Motoyama, H. (2000), *Karma and Reincarnation.* Piatkus

Newton, M. (2012) *Destiny of Souls – New Case Studies of Life Between Lives.* Piatkus

Ogilvie Crombie, R. (2018) *Encounters with Nature Spirits.* Findhorn Press

Steiner, R. (1995) *Manifestations of Karma.* Rudolf Steiner Press

Steiner, R. (1985) *Reincarnation and Karma–Their Significance in Modern Culture.* Rudolf Steiner Press

Steiner, R. (1994) *Theosophy.* Rudolf Steiner Press

Ten Dam, H. (2003) *Exploring Reincarnation.* Rider

Weiss, B. (2012) *Same Soul, Many Bodies.* Piatkus

White, R. (2004) *Working with Spirit Guides.* Piatkus

Woodward, B. (2007) *Spirit Communications.* Athena Press

Woodward, B. (2018) *Trusting in Spirit – The Challenge.* AuthorHouse

Woodward, B. (2020) *Knowledge of Spirit Worlds and Life After Death.* Clairview Books

Woodward, B. (2022) *Journeying into Spirit Worlds.* Clairview Books

MORE ABOUT THE AUTHOR

I was born in 1947 in the UK. At the age of 11, I had the good fortune to fail my 11+ exam, which was then the entrance into what sort of state secondary education was available. Through this stroke of destiny, I entered Wynstones, an independent Rudolf Steiner School in Gloucestershire, where I remained for seven years until I was 18. Following 'A' levels in maths and physics, I went to university, and a year later became a university dropout!

At the age of 23, at Easter 1970, I was guided to become a co-worker at the Sheiling School in Thornbury, a centre of the Camphill Community, based on the teachings of Rudolf Steiner (1861–1925). Apart from a year at Emerson College in Sussex, I spent some 40 years within the Camphill movement, living with and teaching children with special educational needs. I retired from this work in 2012.

I became a student of Steiner's anthroposophy, having first read one of his fundamental books, *Knowledge of the Higher Worlds – How is it Achieved?*, when I was around 18 years old – now more than 50 years ago. Later, I also became a member of the Anthroposophical Society in Great Britain. I have, however, always tried to keep an open mind, and I consider myself a perpetual student. When I was 46, I received a M.Ed. degree from Bristol University and this was followed by a M.Phil. when I was 50. In 2011, I was awarded a Ph.D. from the University of the West of England, when nearly 64.

As well as being a qualified curative educator, I am also a spiritual healer and an author. I took a special interest in understanding autism in children and young people.

I have a lifelong interest in philosophy and spirituality, and in exploring the existential questions of life and death, meaning and freedom. Fundamentally, I see myself as a researcher in the field of spirituality, particularly in my conscious relationships with my spirit guides over the past 17 years, and my ongoing work with them.

In 2022, I will have been married for well over 40 years to my wife, Silke. We have five grown-up children and, currently, ten lively grandchildren. I enjoy walking, swimming, reading, writing, painting and Tai Chi. My wife and I particularly look forward to our holidays in the beautiful Isles of Scilly in Cornwall. I feel that I have received clear guidance in my own life, and am very grateful for this.

Books to challenge C *your perception of reality*

A message from Clairview

We are an independent publishing company with a focus on cutting-edge, non-fiction books. Our innovative list covers current affairs and politics, health, the arts, history, science and spirituality. But regardless of subject, our books have a common link: they all question conventional thinking, dogmas and received wisdom.

Despite being a small company, our list features some big names, such as Booker Prize winner Ben Okri, literary giant Gore Vidal, world leader Mikhail Gorbachev, modern artist Joseph Beuys and natural childbirth pioneer Michel Odent.

So, check out our full catalogue online at
www.clairviewbooks.com
and join our emailing list for news on new titles.

office@clairviewbooks.com

C

CLAIRVIEW